I ♥ SUGAR

Over 100 recipes for people who like it sweet!

LOVE FOOD

Love Food ® is an imprint of Parragon Books Ltd

Parragon
Queen Street House
4 Queen Street
Bath BA1 1HE, UK

Copyright © Parragon Books Ltd 2009
Love Food ® and the accompanying heart device is a trademark of Parragon Books Ltd

ISBN: 978-1-4075-5543-0

Printed in China

Designed by Pink Creative

NOTES FOR THE READER
This book uses imperial, metric, and US cup measurements. Follow the same units of measurement throughout; do not mix imperial and metric. All spoon measurements are level: teaspoons are assumed to be 5 ml, and tablespoons are assumed to be 15 ml. Unless otherwise stated, milk is assumed to be whole, eggs and individual vegetables, such as potatoes, are medium, and pepper is freshly ground black pepper.

The times given are an approximate guide only. Preparation times differ according to the techniques used by different people and the cooking times may also vary from those given as a result of the type of oven used. Optional ingredients, variations, or serving suggestions have not been included in the calculations.

Recipes using raw or very lightly cooked eggs should be avoided by infants, the elderly, pregnant women, convalescents, and anyone with a chronic condition. Pregnant and breastfeeding women are advised to avoid eating peanuts and peanut products. People with nut allergies should be aware that some of the prepared ingredients used in the recipes in this book may contain nuts. Always check the packaging before use.

CONTENTS

INTRODUCTION

If you have a seriously sweet tooth and cannot get by without a daily chocolate fix or contemplate an afternoon cup of coffee without its cookie accompaniment, this is the perfect cookbook for you!

This fantastic collection contains over 100 recipes for all kinds of sweet temptations. Flick through the pages to find irresistible recipes for every occasion—whether you fancy a "little something" between meals, such as a dainty cupcake, or are looking for an indulgent dessert to round off a meal. From comforting fruit pies to brighten up a winter's day to enticing ice creams and sorbets to cool you down when the heat is on, there are dishes for all moods and seasons. In fact, there is so much variety that you are guaranteed to find a recipe to satisfy those sugar cravings, whenever they strike!

YUMMY

Recipes for the chocoholic

CHOCOLATE FUDGE CAKE

Preheat the oven to 350°F/180°C. Grease and line the bottoms of 2 x 8-inch/20-cm round layer cake pans.

To make the frosting, place the chocolate, brown sugar, butter, evaporated milk, and vanilla extract in a heavy-bottom pan. Heat gently, stirring continuously, until melted. Pour into a bowl and let cool. Cover and let chill in the refrigerator for 1 hour, or until spreadable.

Place the butter and superfine sugar in a bowl and beat together until light and fluffy. Gradually beat in the eggs. Stir in the corn syrup and ground almonds. Sift the flour, salt, and cocoa into a separate bowl, then fold into the cake batter. Add a little water, if necessary, to make a dropping consistency.

Spoon the cake batter into the prepared pans and bake in the preheated oven for 30–35 minutes, or until springy to the touch and a skewer inserted in the center comes out clean.

Let stand in the pans for 5 minutes, then turn out onto wire racks to cool completely. When the cakes have cooled, sandwich them together with half the frosting. Spread the remaining frosting over the top and sides of the cake, swirling it to create a decorative appearance.

Serves 8

¾ cup butter, softened, plus extra for greasing

generous 1 cup superfine sugar

3 eggs, beaten

3 tbsp dark corn syrup

3 tbsp ground almonds

generous 1 cup self-rising flour

pinch of salt

¼ cup unsweetened cocoa

Frosting

8 oz/225 g semisweet chocolate, broken into pieces

¼ cup dark brown sugar

1 cup butter, diced

5 tbsp evaporated milk

½ tsp vanilla extract

CHOCOLATE & CHERRY GÂTEAU

Serves 8

2 lb/900 g fresh cherries, pitted and halved

1¼ cups superfine sugar

scant ½ cup cherry brandy

¾ cup all-purpose flour

5 tbsp unsweetened cocoa

½ tsp baking powder

4 eggs

3 tbsp unsalted butter, melted, plus extra for greasing

4 cups heavy cream

2 oz/55 g semisweet chocolate, grated

whole fresh cherries, to decorate

Preheat the oven to 350°F/180°C. Grease and line a 9-inch/23-cm round, springform cake pan.

Place the cherries in a saucepan, add 3 tablespoons of the sugar and the cherry brandy, and bring to a simmer over a medium heat. Simmer for 5 minutes. Drain, reserving the syrup. In a large bowl, sift together the flour, cocoa, and baking powder.

Place the eggs in a heatproof bowl and beat in ¾ cup of the remaining sugar. Place the bowl over a saucepan of simmering water and beat for 6 minutes, or until thickened. Remove from the heat, then gradually fold in the flour mixture and melted butter. Spoon into the prepared cake pan and bake in the preheated oven for 40 minutes. Remove from the oven and let cool in the pan.

Turn out the cake and cut in half horizontally. Mix the cream and the remaining sugar together and whip lightly until soft peaks form. Spread the reserved syrup over the cut sides of the cake, then top with a layer of whipped cream. Arrange the cherry mixture over half of the cake, then place the other half on top. Cover the top of the cake with whipped cream, sprinkle over the grated chocolate, and decorate with the whole fresh cherries.

DOUBLE CHOCOLATE BROWNIES

Preheat the oven to 350°F/180°C. Grease a 7-inch/18-cm square cake pan and line the bottom with parchment paper.

Place the butter and chocolate in a small heatproof bowl set over a saucepan of gently simmering water until melted. Stir until smooth. Let cool slightly. Stir in the sugar, salt, and vanilla extract. Add the eggs, one at a time, stirring well, until blended.

Sift the flour and cocoa into the cake batter and beat until smooth. Stir in the chocolate chips, then pour the batter into the prepared pan. Bake in the preheated oven for 35–40 minutes, or until the top is evenly colored and a toothpick inserted into the center comes out almost clean. Let cool slightly while you prepare the sauce.

To make the sauce, place the butter, sugar, milk, cream, and corn syrup in a small saucepan and heat gently until the sugar has dissolved. Bring to a boil and stir for 10 minutes, or until the mixture is a caramel color. Remove from the heat and add the chocolate. Stir until smooth. Cut the brownies into squares and serve immediately with the sauce.

Makes 9

½ cup butter, plus extra for greasing

4 oz/115 g semisweet chocolate, broken into pieces

1⅓ cups superfine sugar

pinch of salt

1 tsp vanilla extract

2 eggs

1 cup all-purpose flour

2 tbsp unsweetened cocoa

½ cup white chocolate chips

Fudge sauce

4 tbsp butter

generous 1 cup superfine sugar

⅔ cup milk

generous 1 cup heavy cream

⅔ cup dark corn syrup

7 oz/200 g semisweet chocolate, broken into pieces

14

CHEESECAKE BROWNIES

Makes 12

¾ cup unsalted butter, plus extra for greasing

3 tbsp unsweetened cocoa

1 cup superfine sugar

2 eggs, beaten

1 cup all-purpose flour

Cheesecake mix

1 cup ricotta cheese

3 tbsp superfine sugar

1 egg, beaten

Preheat the oven to 350°F/180°C. Grease an 11 x 7-inch/ 28 x 18-cm cake pan and line with parchment paper.

Melt the butter in a medium saucepan, remove from the heat, and stir in the cocoa and sugar. Beat in the eggs, then add the flour and stir to mix evenly. Pour into the prepared pan.

For the cheesecake mix, beat together the ricotta, sugar, and egg, then drop teaspoonfuls of the mixture over the chocolate mixture. Use a metal spatula to swirl the two mixtures lightly together.

Bake in the preheated oven for 40–45 minutes, until just firm to the touch. Cool in the pan, then cut into bars or squares.

DOUBLE CHOCOLATE MUFFINS

Preheat the oven to 375°F/190°C. Place 12 paper liners in a muffin pan.

Put the butter, superfine sugar, and brown sugar into a bowl and beat well. Beat in the eggs, sour cream, and milk until thoroughly mixed. Sift the flour, baking soda, and cocoa into a separate bowl and stir into the mixture. Add the chocolate chips and mix well.

Spoon the batter into the paper liners. Bake in the preheated oven for 25–30 minutes. Remove from the oven and let cool for 10 minutes. Turn out onto a wire rack and let cool completely.

Makes 12

scant ½ cup butter, softened

scant ¾ cup superfine sugar

½ cup dark brown sugar

2 eggs

⅔ cup sour cream

5 tbsp milk

2 cups all-purpose flour

1 tsp baking soda

2 tbsp unsweetened cocoa

1 cup semisweet chocolate chips

CHOCOLATE BUTTERFLY CAKES

Makes 12

½ cup butter

½ cup superfine sugar

1¼ cups self-rising flour

2 eggs

2 tbsp unsweetened cocoa

1 oz/25 g semisweet chocolate, melted

confectioners' sugar, for dusting

Lemon buttercream

6 tbsp butter, softened

1⅓ cups confectioners' sugar, sifted

grated rind of ½ lemon

1 tbsp lemon juice

Preheat the oven to 350°F/180°C. Place 12 paper liners in a shallow muffin pan.

Place the butter, superfine sugar, flour, eggs, and cocoa in a large bowl and beat with an electric mixer until the mixture is just smooth. Beat in the melted chocolate.

Spoon the batter into the paper liners, filling them three-quarters full. Bake in the preheated oven for 15 minutes, or until springy to the touch. Transfer to a wire rack and let cool.

Meanwhile, make the lemon buttercream. Place the butter in a mixing bowl and beat until fluffy, then gradually beat in the confectioners' sugar. Beat in the lemon rind and gradually add the lemon juice, beating well.

Cut the tops off the cakes using a serrated knife. Cut each cake top in half. Spread or pipe the buttercream over the cut surface of each cake and push the 2 cut pieces of cake top into the buttercream to form wings. Dust with confectioners' sugar.

DEVIL'S FOOD CAKES WITH CHOCOLATE FROSTING

Preheat the oven to 350°F/180°C. Put 18 paper liners in a muffin pan, or put 18 double-layer paper liners on a baking sheet.

Put the margarine, brown sugar, eggs, flour, baking soda, and cocoa in a large bowl and, using a handheld electric mixer, beat together until just smooth. Using a metal spoon, fold in the sour cream. Spoon the batter into the paper liners.

Bake the cupcakes in the preheated oven for 20 minutes, or until well risen and firm to the touch. Transfer to a wire rack to cool.

To make the frosting, break the chocolate into a heatproof bowl. Set the bowl over a saucepan of gently simmering water and heat until melted, stirring occasionally. Remove from the heat and let cool slightly, then beat in the sugar and sour cream until combined. Spread the frosting over the tops of the cupcakes and let set in the refrigerator before serving. Serve decorated with chocolate curls.

Makes 18

3½ tbsp soft margarine
½ cup dark brown sugar
2 large eggs
¾ cup all-purpose flour
½ tsp baking soda
¼ cup unsweetened cocoa
½ cup sour cream
chocolate curls, to decorate

Frosting

4½ oz/125 g semisweet chocolate
2 tbsp superfine sugar
⅔ cup sour cream

DOUBLE CHOC COOKIES

Makes about 30

1 cup butter, softened

scant ¾ cup superfine sugar

1 egg yolk, lightly beaten

2 tsp vanilla extract

2¼ cups all-purpose flour

¼ cup unsweetened cocoa

pinch of salt

12 oz/350 g semisweet chocolate, chopped

¼ cup dried sour cherries

Preheat the oven to 375°F/190°C. Line 2 cookie sheets with parchment paper.

Put the butter and sugar into a bowl and mix well with a wooden spoon, then beat in the egg yolk and vanilla extract. Sift together the flour, cocoa, and salt into the mixture, add the chopped chocolate and sour cherries, and stir until thoroughly combined.

Scoop up tablespoons of the mixture and shape into balls. Put them on the prepared cookie sheets, spaced well apart, and flatten slightly.

Bake in the preheated oven for 12–15 minutes. Let cool on the cookie sheets for 5–10 minutes, then carefully transfer to wire racks to cool completely.

CHOCOLATE CARAMEL SHORTBREAD

Preheat the oven to 350°F/180°C. Grease a 9-inch/23-cm square, shallow cake pan and line the bottom with parchment paper.

Place the butter, flour, and sugar in a food processor and process until it starts to bind together. Press into the prepared pan and level the top. Bake in the preheated oven for 20–25 minutes, or until golden.

Meanwhile, make the filling. Place the butter, sugar, corn syrup, and condensed milk in a heavy-bottom saucepan. Heat gently until the sugar has dissolved. Bring to a boil, then reduce the heat and let simmer for 6–8 minutes, stirring, until very thick. Pour over the shortbread and let chill in the refrigerator for 2 hours, or until firm.

Place the chocolate in a heatproof bowl set over a saucepan of gently simmering water and stir until melted. Let cool slightly, then spread over the caramel. Let chill in the refrigerator for 2 hours, or until set. Cut the shortbread into 12 pieces and serve.

Makes 12

½ cup butter, plus extra for greasing

generous 1 cup all-purpose flour

generous ¼ cup superfine sugar

Filling & topping

¾ cup butter

generous ½ cup superfine sugar

3 tbsp dark corn syrup

14 oz/400 g canned sweetened condensed milk

7 oz/200 g semisweet chocolate, broken into pieces

NO-BAKE CHOCOLATE CAKE

Serves 6–8

8 oz/225 g semisweet chocolate

1 cup unsalted butter, plus extra for greasing

3 tbsp black coffee

¼ cup light brown sugar

a few drops of vanilla extract

8 oz/225 g graham crackers, crushed

½ cup raisins

¾ cup walnuts, chopped

Grease an 8 x 4 x 2-inch/20 x 10 x 5-cm loaf pan and line with parchment paper.

Place the chocolate, butter, coffee, sugar, and vanilla extract in a saucepan over low heat and stir until the chocolate and butter have melted, the sugar has dissolved, and the mixture is well combined. Add the crushed crackers, the raisins, and walnuts and stir well.

Spoon the mixture into the prepared loaf pan. Let set and then refrigerate for an hour. When ready to serve, turn out and cut into thin slices.

CHOCOLATE & VANILLA MARBLED LOAF

Preheat the oven to 325°F/160°C. Grease an 8 x 4 x 2-inch/20 x 10 x 5-cm loaf pan and line the bottom with nonstick parchment paper. Dust a little flour around the inside of the pan, shaking out the excess.

Break up the chocolate, place it in a small heatproof bowl with the milk, and set the bowl over a saucepan of simmering water. Heat gently until just melted. Remove from the heat.

Cream together the butter and sugar until light and fluffy. Beat in the egg and sour cream. Sift the flour and baking powder into the mixture, then fold in lightly and evenly using a metal spoon.

Spoon half the batter into a separate bowl and stir in the chocolate mixture. Add the vanilla extract to the plain batter.

Spoon the chocolate and vanilla batters alternately into the prepared loaf pan, swirling lightly with a knife or skewer for a marbled effect. Bake in the preheated oven for 40–45 minutes, or until well risen and firm to the touch.

Cool in the pan for 10 minutes, then turn out and finish cooling on a wire rack.

Serves 8

2 oz/55 g semisweet chocolate

3 tbsp milk

5 tbsp butter, plus extra for greasing

scant ½ cup superfine sugar

1 egg, beaten

3 tbsp sour cream

1 cup self-rising flour, plus extra for dusting

½ tsp baking powder

½ tsp vanilla extract

CHOCOLATE BROWNIE ROULADE

Serves 6

butter, for greasing

5½ oz/150 g semisweet chocolate, broken into pieces

3 tbsp water

¾ cup superfine sugar

5 eggs, separated

2 tbsp raisins, chopped

¼ cup pecans, chopped

pinch of salt

1¼ cups heavy cream, lightly whipped

confectioners' sugar, for dusting

Preheat the oven to 350°F/180°C. Grease a 12 x 8-inch/ 30 x 20-cm jelly roll pan, line with parchment paper, and grease the parchment.

Melt the chocolate with the water in a small pan over low heat until the chocolate has just melted. Let cool.

In a bowl, beat the sugar and egg yolks with a handheld electric mixer for 2–3 minutes, until thick and pale. Fold in the cooled chocolate, the raisins, and pecans.

In a separate bowl, beat the egg whites with the salt. Fold one quarter of the egg whites into the chocolate mixture, then fold in the rest of the whites, working lightly and quickly.

Transfer the mixture to the prepared pan and bake in a preheated oven for 25 minutes, until risen and just firm to the touch. Let cool before covering with a sheet of nonstick parchment paper and a damp, clean dish cloth. Let cool completely.

Turn the roulade out onto another piece of parchment paper dusted with confectioners' sugar and remove the lining paper.

Spread the cream over the roulade. Starting from a short end, roll the sponge away from you using the paper to guide you. Trim the ends of the roulade to make a neat finish and transfer to a serving plate. Let chill in the refrigerator until ready to serve. Dust with a little confectioners' sugar before serving, if desired.

INDIVIDUAL CHOCOLATE SPONGES

Grease 4 x ¾-cup baking dishes.

To make the sponges, put the sugar and eggs into a heatproof bowl and place over a saucepan of simmering water. Whisk for about 10 minutes, until frothy. Remove the bowl from the heat and fold in the flour and cocoa. Fold in the butter, then the chocolate. Mix well.

Spoon the mixture into the prepared baking dishes and cover with parchment paper. Top with foil and secure with string. Place in a large saucepan filled with enough simmering water to reach halfway up the sides of the bowls. Steam for about 40 minutes, or until cooked through.

About 2–3 minutes before the end of the cooking time, make the sauce. Put the butter, chocolate, water, and sugar into a small saucepan and warm over low heat, stirring continuously, until melted and combined. Stir in the liqueur.

Remove the sponges from the heat, turn out onto serving dishes, and pour over the sauce. Decorate with coffee beans and serve.

Serves 4

Sponges
½ cup superfine sugar

3 eggs

½ cup all-purpose flour

½ cup unsweetened cocoa

scant ½ cup unsalted butter, melted, plus extra for greasing

3½ oz/100 g semisweet chocolate, melted

Chocolate sauce
2 tbsp unsalted butter

3½ oz/100 g semisweet chocolate

5 tbsp water

1 tbsp superfine sugar

1 tbsp coffee-flavored liqueur, such as Kahlúa

coffee beans, to decorate

CHOCOLATE CRUMBLE PIE

Serves 8

Pie dough

1¼ cups all-purpose flour

1 tsp baking powder

½ cup unsalted butter, cut into small pieces

¼ cup superfine sugar

1 egg yolk

1–2 tsp cold water

Filling

⅔ cup heavy cream

⅔ cup milk

8 oz/225 g semisweet chocolate, chopped

2 eggs

Crumble topping

¾ cup toasted pecans

4 oz/115 g semisweet chocolate

3 oz/85 g amaretti cookies

½ cup light brown sugar

1 tsp unsweetened cocoa

To make the pie dough, sift the flour and baking powder into a large bowl, rub in the butter, and stir in the sugar, then add the egg and a little water to bring the dough together. Turn the dough out and knead briefly. Wrap and let chill in the refrigerator for 30 minutes.

Preheat the oven to 375°F/190°C. Roll out the pie dough and use to line a 9-inch/23-cm round, loose-bottom tart pan. Prick the pastry shell with a fork. Line with parchment paper and fill with dried beans. Bake in the preheated oven for 15 minutes. Remove from the oven and take out the paper and beans. Reduce the oven temperature to 350°F/180°C.

For the filling, bring the cream and milk to a boil in a saucepan, remove from the heat, and add the chocolate. Stir until melted and smooth. Beat the eggs and add to the chocolate mixture, mix thoroughly, and pour into the pastry shell. Bake for 15 minutes, remove from the oven, and let rest for 1 hour.

When you are ready to serve the pie, chop the pecans and chocolate with a large knife and crush the cookies. Place in a large bowl, then add the sugar and cocoa and mix well. Sprinkle over the pie, cut into slices, and serve.

MISSISSIPPI MUD PIE

Preheat the oven to 350°F/180°C. Lightly grease a 23-cm/9-inch round, loose-bottom cake pan.

To make the crumb crust, put the graham crackers, pecans, sugar, and cinnamon into a food processor and process until fine crumbs form – do not overprocess to a powder. Add the melted butter and process again until moistened.

Turn the crumb mixture into the prepared cake pan and press over the bottom and about 1½ inches/4 cm up the sides of the pan. Cover the pan and chill while you make the filling.

To make the filling, put the butter, chocolate, and corn syrup into a saucepan over low heat and stir until melted and blended. Let cool, then beat in the eggs and pecans.

Pour the filling into the chilled crumb crust and smooth the surface. Bake in the preheated oven for 30 minutes, or until just set but still soft in the center. Let cool on a wire rack. Serve at room temperature or chilled.

Serves 12–14

Crumb crust
5 oz/140 g graham crackers

½ cup pecans, finely chopped

1 tbsp light brown sugar

½ tsp ground cinnamon

6 tbsp butter, melted, plus extra for greasing

Filling
1 cup butter or margarine

6 oz/175 g semisweet chocolate, chopped

½ cup dark corn syrup

4 large eggs, beaten

½ cup pecans, finely chopped

Serves 6–8

Crumb crust

4 oz/115 g graham crackers, finely crushed

2 tsp unsweetened cocoa

4 tbsp butter, melted, plus extra for greasing

Chocolate layer

1 lb 12 oz/800 g mascarpone cheese

1½ cups confectioners' sugar, sifted

juice of ½ orange

finely grated rind of 1 orange

6 oz/175 g semisweet chocolate

2 tbsp brandy

chocolate leaves, to decorate

DEEP CHOCOLATE CHEESECAKE

Grease an 8-inch/20-cm round, loose-bottom cake pan.

To make the crumb crust, put the graham crackers, cocoa, and melted butter into a large bowl and mix well. Press the crumb mixture evenly over the bottom of the prepared pan.

For the chocolate layer, put the mascarpone cheese and sugar into a bowl and stir in the orange juice and rind. Place the chocolate in a heatproof bowl set over a saucepan of gently simmering water until melted. Let cool slightly, then stir in the brandy. Add to the mascarpone cheese mixture and mix together until thoroughly combined. Spread the chocolate mixture evenly over the crumb crust. Cover with plastic wrap and chill for at least 4 hours.

Remove the cheesecake from the refrigerator, turn out onto a serving platter, and decorate with chocolate leaves. Serve immediately.

CREAM PUFFS WITH CHOCOLATE SAUCE

Preheat the oven to 400°F/200°C. Grease a large baking sheet.

To make the choux pastry, place the butter and water in a saucepan and bring to a boil. Meanwhile, sift the flour into a bowl. Turn off the heat and beat in the flour until smooth. Cool for 5 minutes. Beat in enough of the eggs to give the mixture a soft, dropping consistency.

Transfer to a pastry bag fitted with a ½-inch/1-cm plain tip. Pipe small balls onto the baking sheet. Bake in the preheated oven for 25 minutes.

Remove from the oven. Pierce each ball with a skewer to let the steam escape.

To make the filling, whip the cream, sugar, and vanilla extract together. Cut the balls across the middle, then fill with the cream mixture.

To make the sauce, gently melt the chocolate, butter, and water together in a small saucepan, stirring constantly, until smooth. Stir in the cognac.

Pile the cream puffs onto individual serving dishes. Pour over the sauce and serve.

Serves 4

Choux pastry

5 tbsp butter, plus extra for greasing

scant 1 cup water

¾ cup all-purpose flour

3 eggs, beaten

Cream filling

1¼ cups heavy cream

3 tbsp superfine sugar

1 tsp vanilla extract

Chocolate sauce

4½ oz/125 g semisweet chocolate, broken into small pieces

2½ tbsp butter

6 tbsp water

2 tbsp cognac

CHOCOLATE MOUSSE

Serves 4–6

8 oz/225 g semisweet chocolate, chopped

2 tbsp cognac, Grand Marnier, or Cointreau

4 tbsp water

2 tbsp unsalted butter, diced

3 large eggs, separated

¼ tsp cream of tartar

¼ cup superfine sugar

½ cup heavy cream

Place the chocolate, cognac, and water in a small pan over low heat and melt, stirring, until smooth. Remove the pan from the heat and beat in the butter.

Beat the egg yolks into the chocolate mixture, one after another, until blended, then let cool slightly.

Meanwhile, using an electric mixer on low speed, beat the egg whites in a spotlessly clean bowl until they are frothy, then gradually increase the mixer's speed and beat until soft peaks form. Sprinkle the cream of tartar over the surface, then add the sugar, tablespoon by tablespoon, and continue beating until stiff peaks form. Beat several tablespoons of the egg whites into the chocolate mixture to loosen.

In another bowl, whip the cream until soft peaks form. Spoon the cream over the chocolate mixture, then spoon the remaining whites over the cream. Use a large metal spoon to fold the chocolate into the cream and egg whites.

Divide the mousse among 4–6 individual serving bowls. Cover the bowls with plastic wrap and chill for at least 3 hours before serving.

CHOCOLATE ICE-CREAM BITES

Line a cookie sheet with plastic wrap.

Using a melon baller, scoop out balls of ice cream and place them on the prepared cookie sheet. Alternatively, cut the ice cream into bite-size cubes. Stick a toothpick in each piece and return to the freezer until very hard.

Place the chocolate and the butter in a heatproof bowl set over a pan of gently simmering water until melted. Quickly dip the frozen ice-cream balls into the warm chocolate, place in a paper muffin liner, and return to the freezer to set. Keep them there until ready to serve.

Serves 6

2½ cups good-quality ice cream

7 oz/200 g semisweet chocolate

2 tbsp unsalted butter

CHOCOLATE ICE CREAM

Serves 4–6

1¼ cups milk

1 vanilla bean

3½ oz/100 g semisweet chocolate

3 egg yolks

scant ½ cup superfine sugar

1¼ cups heavy cream

Pour the milk into a large, heavy-bottom pan. Split open the vanilla bean and scrape out the seeds into the milk, then add the whole vanilla bean. Bring almost to a boil, then remove from the heat and let stand for 30 minutes. Remove the vanilla bean from the milk. Break the chocolate into the milk and heat gently, stirring constantly until melted and smooth.

Put the egg yolks and sugar in a large bowl and beat together until pale and the mixture leaves a trail when the beaters are lifted. Gradually add the chocolate mixture, stirring constantly with a wooden spoon. Strain the mixture into the rinsed out pan or a double boiler and cook over low heat for 10–15 minutes, stirring constantly, until the mixture thickens enough to coat the back of a wooden spoon. Do not let the mixture boil or it will curdle. Remove the custard from the heat and let cool for at least 1 hour, stirring occasionally to prevent a skin from forming. Meanwhile, whip the cream until it holds its shape. Set aside in the refrigerator until ready to use.

If using an ice-cream machine, fold the whipped cream into the cold custard, then churn the mixture in the machine following the manufacturer's instructions. Alternatively, freeze the custard in a freezerproof container, uncovered, for 1–2 hours, or until it begins to set around the edges. Turn the custard into a bowl and stir with a fork or beat in a food processor until smooth. Fold in the whipped cream. Return to the freezer and freeze for an additional 2–3 hours, or until firm. Cover the container with a lid for storing.

CHOCOLATE CREAMS

Line a cookie sheet with parchment paper.

Melt one third of the chocolate in a large heatproof bowl set over a saucepan of gently simmering water. Stir in the cream and remove the bowl from the heat.

Sift the confectioners' sugar into the melted chocolate then, using a fork, mix well together. Knead to form a firm, smooth, pliable mixture.

Lightly dust a counter with cocoa, turn out the mixture, and roll out to a thickness of ¼ inch/ 5 mm, then cut into circles, using a 1-inch/2.5-cm plain, round cutter.

Transfer to the prepared cookie sheet and let stand for about 12 hours or overnight, until set and dry.

When the chocolate creams have set, line a cookie sheet with parchment paper. Melt the remaining chocolate in a heatproof bowl set over a saucepan of gently simmering water. Using 2 forks, carefully dip each chocolate cream into the melted chocolate. Lift out quickly, letting any excess chocolate drip back into the bowl, and place on the prepared cookie sheet. Let set.

Makes about 30

7 oz/200 g semisweet chocolate, broken into pieces

2 tbsp light cream

2 cups confectioners' sugar

unsweetened cocoa, for dusting

WHITE CHOCOLATE TRUFFLES

Makes 20

2 tbsp unsalted butter

5 tbsp heavy cream

11½ oz/325 g white chocolate, broken into pieces

1 tbsp orange liqueur (optional)

Line a jelly roll pan with parchment paper.

Place the butter and cream in a small saucepan and bring slowly to a boil, stirring constantly. Boil for 1 minute, then remove from the heat.

Add two thirds of the chocolate to the cream. Stir until melted, then beat in the liqueur, if using. Pour into the prepared pan and chill for about 2 hours, until firm.

Break off pieces of the mixture and roll them into balls. Chill for an additional 30 minutes before finishing the truffles.

To finish, put the remaining chocolate in a heatproof bowl set over a saucepan of gently simmering water until melted. Dip the balls in the chocolate, letting any excess chocolate drip back into the bowl. Place on parchment paper, swirl the chocolate with the tines of a fork, and let set.

ITALIAN CHOCOLATE TRUFFLES

Melt the semisweet chocolate with the amaretto in a heatproof bowl set over a saucepan of hot water, stirring until well combined.

Add the butter and stir until it has melted. Stir in the confectioners' sugar and the ground almonds.

Let the mixture stand in a cool place until it is firm enough to roll into 24 balls.

Place the grated chocolate on a plate and roll the truffles in the chocolate to coat them.

Place the truffles in candy paper liners and let chill.

Makes 24

6 oz/175 g semisweet chocolate

2 tbsp amaretto or orange liqueur

3 tbsp unsalted butter

4 tbsp confectioners' sugar

½ cup ground almonds

1¾ oz/50 g semisweet chocolate, grated

ROCKY ROAD BITES

Makes 18

4½ oz/125 g milk chocolate

1¾ oz/50 g mini marshmallows

¼ cup chopped walnuts

2 tbsp chopped, plumped dried apricots

Line a cookie sheet with parchment paper.

Break the chocolate into small pieces and place in a large, heatproof bowl. Set the bowl over a saucepan of gently simmering water and stir until the chocolate has melted.

Stir in the marshmallows, walnuts, and apricots, and toss in the melted chocolate until well covered.

Place heaping teaspoons of the marshmallow mixture onto the prepared cookie sheet, then let chill in the refrigerator until set.

Once they are set, carefully remove from the parchment paper. Place in candy paper liners to serve, if desired.

CHOCOLATE FONDUE

Using a sharp knife, peel and core the pineapple, then cut the flesh into cubes. Peel the mango, remove the pit, and cut the flesh into cubes. Arrange all the fruit on 6 serving plates and let chill in the refrigerator.

To make the fondue, place the chocolate and cream in a fondue pot. Heat gently, stirring constantly, until the chocolate has melted. Stir in the cognac until thoroughly blended and the chocolate mixture is smooth.

Place the fondue pot over the burner to keep warm. To serve, let each guest dip the fruit into the fondue, using fondue forks or bamboo skewers.

Serves 6

1 pineapple

1 mango

9 oz/250 g fresh strawberries

9 oz/250 g seedless green grapes

Fondue

9 oz/250 g semisweet chocolate, broken into pieces

⅔ cup heavy cream

2 tbsp cognac

HOT CHOCOLATE FLOAT

Serves 4

2 cups milk

8 oz/225 g semisweet chocolate

2 tbsp superfine sugar

8 scoops coconut ice cream

8 scoops chocolate ice cream

whipped cream, to decorate

Pour the milk into a saucepan. Break the chocolate into pieces and add to the saucepan with the sugar. Stir over low heat until the chocolate has melted, the sugar has dissolved, and the mixture is smooth. Remove the saucepan from the heat.

Put 1 scoop of coconut ice cream into each of 4 heatproof glasses, top with a scoop of chocolate ice cream, then repeat the layers.

Pour the chocolate-flavored milk into the glasses, top with whipped cream, and serve immediately.

SCRUMPTIOUS

Cakes for all occasions

FROSTED CUPCAKES

Preheat the oven to 375°F/190°C. Place 16 paper liners in a shallow muffin pan.

Place the butter and superfine sugar in a large bowl and cream together with a wooden spoon or electric mixer until pale and fluffy.

Gradually add the eggs, beating well after each addition. Fold in the flour lightly and evenly using a metal spoon.

Divide the batter among the paper liners and bake in the preheated oven for 15–20 minutes. Cool on a wire rack.

For the frosting, sift the confectioners' sugar into a bowl and stir in just enough of the water to mix to a smooth paste that is thick enough to coat the back of a wooden spoon. Stir in a few drops of food coloring, if using. Spread the frosting over the cupcakes and decorate as desired.

Makes 16
½ cup butter, softened

generous ½ cup superfine sugar

2 eggs, beaten

1 cup self-rising flour

Frosting & decoration
1¾ cups confectioners' sugar

about 2 tbsp warm water

a few drops of edible food coloring (optional)

sugar flowers, sprinkles, and/or candied cherries, to decorate

RASPBERRY ALMOND CUPCAKES

Makes 14

½ cup butter, softened

scant ½ cup superfine sugar

½ tsp almond extract

2 eggs, lightly beaten

scant ⅔ cup self-rising flour

scant ⅔ cup ground almonds

85 g/3 oz fresh raspberries

2 tbsp slivered almonds

confectioners' sugar,
for dusting

Preheat the oven to 350°F/180°C. Place 14 paper liners in a shallow muffin pan.

Put the butter, sugar, and almond extract in a bowl and beat together until light and fluffy. Gradually beat in the eggs. Sift in the flour and, using a metal spoon, fold into the mixture with the ground almonds. Gently fold in the raspberries. Spoon the mixture into the paper liners. Scatter the slivered almonds over the top.

Bake the cupcakes in the preheated oven for 25–30 minutes, or until golden brown and firm to the touch. Transfer to a wire rack and let cool. Dust with confectioners' sugar.

MACADAMIA & MAPLE CUPCAKES

Preheat the oven to 375°F/190°C. Put 10 paper liners in a shallow muffin pan.

Put the butter, brown sugar, and maple syrup in a bowl and beat together until light and fluffy. Gradually beat in the egg. Sift in the flour and, using a metal spoon, fold into the mixture with the nuts and milk. Spoon the mixture into the paper liners.

Bake the cupcakes in the preheated oven for 20 minutes, or until golden brown and firm to the touch. Transfer to a wire rack and let cool.

To make the frosting, beat the butter and maple syrup together until smooth. Sift in the confectioners' sugar and beat in thoroughly. Gently beat in the cream cheese. Swirl the frosting on the top of each cake and sprinkle over the toasted nuts.

Makes 10

6 tbsp butter, softened
¼ cup light brown sugar
2 tbsp maple syrup
1 large egg, lightly beaten
⅔ cup self-rising flour
½ cup macadamia nuts, chopped
1 tbsp milk

Frosting

2 tbsp butter, softened
2 tbsp maple syrup
¾ cup confectioners' sugar
⅓ cup cream cheese
2 tbsp chopped macadamia nuts, lightly toasted

SPICED PLUM CUPCAKES

Makes 4

4 tbsp butter, softened, plus extra for greasing

generous ¼ cup superfine sugar

1 large egg, lightly beaten

generous ⅓ cup all-purpose whole wheat flour

½ tsp baking powder

1 tsp ground allspice

¼ cup coarsely ground, blanched hazelnuts

2 small plums, halved, pitted, and sliced

Preheat the oven to 350°F/180°C. Grease 4 x ⅔-cup ovenproof dishes (such as ramekins) with butter.

Put the butter and sugar in a bowl and beat together until light and fluffy. Gradually beat in the egg. Sift in the flour, baking powder, and allspice (tipping any bran left in the sifter into the bowl) and, using a metal spoon, fold into the mixture with the ground hazelnuts. Spoon the mixture into the dishes. Arrange the sliced plums on top of the mixture.

Put the dishes on a baking sheet and bake in the preheated oven for 25 minutes, or until risen and firm to the touch. Serve warm or cold.

LOW-FAT BLUEBERRY MUFFINS

Preheat the oven to 375°F/190°C. Place 12 paper liners in a muffin pan.

Sift the flour, baking soda, salt, and half of the allspice into a large mixing bowl. Add 6 tablespoons of the superfine sugar and mix together.

In a separate bowl, whisk the egg whites together. Add the margarine, yogurt, and vanilla extract and mix together well, then stir in the blueberries until thoroughly mixed. Add to the flour mixture, then gently stir together until just combined. Do not overstir the batter—it is fine for it to be a little lumpy.

Divide the muffin batter evenly among the paper liners (they should be about two-thirds full). Mix the remaining sugar with the remaining allspice, then sprinkle the mixture over the muffins.

Bake in the preheated oven for 25 minutes, or until risen and golden. Remove the muffins from the oven and serve warm, or place them on a wire rack and let cool.

Makes 12

generous 1½ cups all-purpose flour

1 tsp baking soda

¼ tsp salt

1 tsp allspice

generous ½ cup superfine sugar

3 egg whites

3 tbsp low-fat margarine

⅔ cup thick low-fat plain yogurt or blueberry-flavored yogurt

1 tsp vanilla extract

¾ cup fresh blueberries

LEMON & POPPY SEED MUFFINS

Makes 12

3 cups all-purpose flour

1 tbsp baking powder

generous ½ cup superfine sugar

2 tbsp poppy seeds

4 tbsp butter

1 extra-large egg, beaten

1 cup milk

finely grated rind and juice of 1 lemon

Preheat the oven to 375°F/190°C. Place 12 paper liners in a muffin pan.

Sift the flour and baking powder into a large bowl and stir in the sugar.

Heat a heavy skillet over medium–high heat and add the poppy seeds. Toast the poppy seeds for about 30 seconds, shaking the skillet to prevent them from burning. Remove from the heat and add to the flour mixture.

Melt the butter, then beat with the egg, milk, lemon rind, and lemon juice. Pour into the dry mixture and stir well to mix evenly to a soft, sticky dough. Add a little more milk if the mixture is too dry.

Spoon the batter into the paper liners, then bake in the preheated oven for 25–30 minutes, or until risen and golden brown. Lift onto a wire rack to cool.

JELLY DOUGHNUT MUFFINS

Preheat the oven to 400°F/200°C. Grease a 12-cup muffin pan or line with 12 paper liners.

Sift together the flour, baking powder, and salt into a large bowl. Stir in the sugar.

Lightly beat the eggs in a large pitcher or bowl, then beat in the milk, oil, and vanilla extract. Make a well in the center of the dry ingredients and pour in the beaten liquid ingredients. Stir gently until just combined; do not overmix.

Spoon half the batter into the prepared muffin pan. Add a teaspoon of jelly to the center of each, then spoon in the remaining batter. Bake in the preheated oven for about 20 minutes, until well risen, golden brown, and firm to the touch.

Meanwhile, make the topping. Melt the butter. Spread the sugar in a wide, shallow bowl. When the muffins are baked, let them cool in the pan for 5 minutes. Dip the tops of the muffins in the melted butter then roll in the sugar. Serve warm or transfer to a wire rack and let cool completely.

Makes 12

oil or melted butter, for greasing (if using)

2 cups all-purpose flour

1 tbsp baking powder

⅛ tsp salt

generous ½ cup superfine sugar

2 large eggs

scant 1 cup milk

6 tbsp sunflower oil or melted, cooled butter

1 tsp vanilla extract

4 tbsp strawberry jelly or raspberry jelly

Topping

½ cup butter

generous ¾ cup sugar

TROPICAL FRUIT MUFFINS

Makes 12

oil or melted butter,
for greasing (if using)

2 bananas

about ⅔ cup milk

2 cups all-purpose flour

1 tbsp baking powder

⅛ tsp salt

generous ½ cup light brown sugar

2 large eggs

6 tbsp sunflower oil or melted, cooled butter

1 tsp vanilla extract

2 passion fruits

2 tbsp honey

Preheat the oven to 400°F/200°C. Grease a 12-cup muffin pan or line with 12 paper liners.

Mash the bananas and put in a measuring cup. Add enough milk to the puree to make up to 1 cup.

Sift together the flour, baking powder, and salt into a large bowl. Stir in the sugar.

Lightly beat the eggs in a large pitcher or bowl, then beat in the banana-and-milk mixture, the oil, and vanilla extract. Make a well in the center of the dry ingredients and pour in the beaten liquid ingredients. Stir gently until just combined; do not overmix.

Spoon the batter into the prepared muffin pan. Bake in the preheated oven for about 20 minutes, until well risen, golden brown, and firm to the touch.

Let the muffins cool in the pan for 5 minutes, then transfer to a wire rack and let cool completely.

Meanwhile, halve the passion fruits and spoon the pulp into a small saucepan. Add the honey and heat very gently until warmed through. Spoon on top of the muffins before serving.

SPONGE LAYER CAKE

Preheat the oven to 350°F/180°C. Grease 2 x 8-inch/20-cm round layer cake pans and line with parchment paper.

Cream the butter and superfine sugar together in a mixing bowl using a wooden spoon or a handheld mixer until the mixture is pale in color and light and fluffy. Add the eggs, one at a time, beating well after each addition.

Sift the flour and salt together into a separate bowl and carefully add to the mixture, folding it in with a metal spoon or a spatula. Divide the mixture between the prepared pans and smooth over with a spatula.

Place the pans in the center of the oven and bake in the preheated oven for 25–30 minutes, until well risen, golden brown, and beginning to shrink from the sides of the pan.

Remove from the oven and let stand for 1 minute. Loosen the cakes from around the edges of the pans using a palette knife. Turn the cakes out onto a clean dish towel, remove the paper, and invert the cakes onto a wire rack.

When completely cool, sandwich together the cakes with the jelly and sprinkle with the sugar.

Serves 8–10

¾ cup unsalted butter, at room temperature, plus extra for greasing

¾ cup superfine sugar

3 eggs, beaten

scant 1½ cups self-rising flour

pinch of salt

3 tbsp raspberry jelly

1 tbsp superfine or confectioners' sugar

COFFEE & WALNUT CAKE

Serves 8

¾ cup butter, plus extra
for greasing

¾ cup light brown sugar

3 extra-large eggs, beaten

3 tbsp strong black coffee

1½ cups self-rising flour

1½ tsp baking powder

1 cup walnut pieces

walnut halves, to decorate

Frosting

½ cup butter

1¾ cups confectioners' sugar

1 tbsp strong black coffee

½ tsp vanilla extract

Preheat the oven to 350°F/180°C. Grease and line the bottoms of 2 x 8-inch/20-cm round layer cake pans.

Cream together the butter and brown sugar until pale and fluffy. Gradually add the eggs, beating well after each addition. Beat in the coffee.

Sift the flour and baking powder into the mixture, then fold in lightly and evenly with a metal spoon. Fold in the walnut pieces.

Divide the batter between the prepared cake pans and smooth level. Bake in the preheated oven for 20–25 minutes, or until golden brown and springy to the touch. Turn out onto a wire rack to cool.

For the frosting, beat together the butter, confectioners' sugar, coffee, and vanilla extract, mixing until smooth and creamy.

Use about half of the frosting to sandwich the cakes together, then spread the remaining frosting on top and swirl with a metal spatula. Decorate with walnut halves.

CLASSIC CHERRY CAKE

Preheat the oven to 350°F/180°C. Grease an 8-inch/20-cm round cake pan and line the bottom with parchment paper.

Stir together the candied cherries, ground almonds, and 1 tablespoon of the flour. Sift the remaining flour into a separate bowl with the baking powder.

Cream together the butter and sugar until light in color and fluffy in texture. Gradually add the eggs, beating hard with each addition, until evenly mixed.

Add the flour mixture and fold lightly and evenly into the creamed mixture with a metal spoon. Add the cherry mixture and fold in evenly. Finally, fold in the lemon rind and juice.

Spoon the batter into the prepared cake pan and sprinkle with the crushed sugar cubes. Bake in the preheated oven for 1–1¼ hours, or until risen, golden brown, and the cake is just beginning to shrink away from the sides of the pan.

Cool in the pan for about 15 minutes, then turn out to finish cooling on a wire rack.

Serves 8

generous 1 cup candied cherries, quartered

¾ cup ground almonds

1¾ cups all-purpose flour

1 tsp baking powder

scant 1 cup butter, plus extra for greasing

1 cup superfine sugar

3 extra-large eggs

finely grated rind and juice of 1 lemon

6 sugar cubes, crushed

JEWEL-TOPPED POUND CAKE

Serves 8–10

1 cup butter, softened, plus extra for greasing

generous 1 cup superfine sugar

finely grated rind of 1 lemon

4 eggs, beaten

2½ cups self-rising flour, sifted

2–3 tbsp milk

Fruit topping

2½ tbsp honey

1½ cups candied fruit

Preheat the oven to 325°F/160°C. Grease an 8-inch/20-cm round, deep cake pan and line the bottom with parchment paper.

Put the butter, sugar, and lemon rind in a bowl and beat together until light and fluffy. Gradually beat in the eggs. Gently fold in the flour, alternately with enough milk to create a soft, dropping consistency.

Spoon the batter into the prepared pan and bake in the preheated oven for 1½–1¾ hours, until risen and golden and a skewer inserted into the center comes out clean.

Let cool in the pan for 10 minutes, then turn out, remove the paper, and place on a wire rack to cool. To make the topping, brush the honey over the cake and arrange the fruit on top.

PINEAPPLE UPSIDE-DOWN CAKE

Preheat the oven to 325°F/160°C. Grease a 9-inch/23-cm round, deep cake pan with a solid bottom and line the bottom with parchment paper.

For the topping, place the butter and corn syrup in a heavy-bottom pan and heat gently until melted. Bring to a boil and boil for 2–3 minutes, stirring, until slightly thickened and taffylike.

Pour the syrup into the bottom of the prepared pan. Arrange the pineapple rings and candied cherries in a single layer over the syrup.

Place the eggs, sugar, and vanilla extract in a large, heatproof bowl set over a saucepan of gently simmering water and beat with an electric mixer for 10–15 minutes, until thick enough to leave a trail when the beaters are lifted. Sift in the flour and baking powder and fold in lightly and evenly with a metal spoon.

Fold the melted butter into the mixture with a metal spoon until evenly mixed. Spoon into the prepared pan and bake in the preheated oven for 1–1¼ hours, or until well risen, firm, and golden brown.

Let cool in the pan for 10 minutes, then carefully turn out onto a serving plate. Serve warm or cold.

Serves 10

4 eggs, beaten

1 cup superfine sugar

1 tsp vanilla extract

1¾ cups all-purpose flour

2 tsp baking powder

generous ½ cup unsalted butter, melted, plus extra for greasing

Topping

3 tbsp unsalted butter

4 tbsp dark corn syrup

15 oz/425 g canned pineapple rings, drained

4–6 candied cherries, halved

APPLE STREUSEL CAKE

Serves 8

1 lb 2 oz/500 g apples, peeled, cored, and cut into ½-inch/1-cm dice

1 tbsp lemon juice

generous ½ cup unsalted butter, plus extra for greasing

⅔ cup superfine sugar

2 extra-large eggs, beaten

2 cups all-purpose flour

3 tsp baking powder

1 tsp ground cinnamon

½ tsp ground nutmeg

3 tbsp hard cider or apple juice

Streusel topping

⅓ cup hazelnuts, skinned and finely chopped

⅓ cup all-purpose flour

2 tbsp light brown sugar

½ tsp ground cinnamon

2 tbsp unsalted butter, melted

Preheat the oven to 350°F/180°C. Grease an 8 inch/20-cm round, loose-bottom cake pan and line the bottom with parchment paper. Toss the apples in the lemon juice.

Cream together the butter and superfine sugar until pale and fluffy, then gradually add the eggs, beating thoroughly after each addition. Sift the flour, baking powder, cinnamon, and nutmeg into the mixture and fold in lightly and evenly using a metal spoon. Stir in the hard cider.

Stir the apples into the batter to distribute evenly, then spoon into the prepared pan and level the surface.

For the streusel topping, combine the hazelnuts, flour, brown sugar, and cinnamon, then stir in the melted butter, mixing until crumbly. Spread over the cake.

Bake the cake in the preheated oven for 1–1¼ hours, or until firm and golden brown. Let cool for 10 minutes in the pan, then remove carefully and finish cooling on a wire rack.

HONEY & ALMOND CAKE

Preheat the oven to 350°F/180°C. Grease a 7-inch/18-cm round cake pan and line with parchment paper.

Place the margarine, brown sugar, eggs, flour, baking powder, milk, and honey in a large mixing bowl and beat well with a wooden spoon for about 1 minute, until all of the ingredients are thoroughly mixed together.

Spoon into the prepared pan, smooth the surface with the back of a spoon or a knife, and sprinkle with the almonds.

Bake in the preheated oven for about 50 minutes, or until the cake is well risen and a skewer inserted into the center comes out clean.

Meanwhile, make the syrup. Combine the honey and lemon juice in a small pan and simmer over low heat for about 5 minutes, or until the syrup coats the back of a spoon.

As soon as the cake comes out of the oven, pour over the syrup, letting it seep into the middle of the cake.

Let the cake cool for at least 2 hours before slicing.

Serves 8

⅓ cup soft margarine, plus extra for greasing

¼ cup light brown sugar

2 eggs

1¼ cups self-rising flour

1 tsp baking powder

4 tbsp milk

2 tbsp honey

½ cup slivered almonds

Syrup

⅔ cup honey

2 tbsp lemon juice

BANANA & CRANBERRY LOAF

Serves 8–10

butter, for greasing

1½ cups self-rising flour

½ tsp baking powder

1 cup light brown sugar

2 bananas, mashed

¼ cup chopped mixed peel

⅓ cup chopped mixed nuts

⅓ cup dried cranberries

5–6 tbsp orange juice

2 eggs, beaten

⅔ cup sunflower oil

⅔ cup confectioners' sugar, sifted

grated rind of 1 orange

Preheat the oven to 350°F/180°C. Grease a 9 x 5 x 3-inch/ 23 x 13 x 8-cm loaf pan and line the bottom with parchment paper.

Sift the flour and baking powder into a large mixing bowl. Stir in the brown sugar, bananas, mixed peel, nuts, and cranberries.

Stir together the orange juice, eggs, and oil until well combined, then add the mixture to the dry ingredients and mix until well blended. Pour into the prepared pan.

Bake in the preheated oven for about 1 hour, until firm to the touch and a skewer inserted into the center comes out clean. Turn out onto a wire rack and let cool.

Mix the confectioners' sugar with a little water and drizzle the frosting over the loaf. Sprinkle the orange rind over the top. Let the frosting set before slicing.

ORANGE & POPPY SEED BUNDT CAKE

Preheat the oven to 325°F/160°C. Grease and lightly flour a Bundt tube pan, about 9½ inches/ 24 cm in diameter and with a capacity of approximately 9 cups.

Cream together the butter and sugar until pale and fluffy, then add the eggs gradually, beating thoroughly after each addition. Stir in the orange rind and poppy seeds. Sift in the flour and baking powder, then fold in evenly.

Add the milk and orange juice, stirring to mix evenly. Spoon the batter into the prepared pan and bake in the preheated oven for 45–50 minutes, or until firm and golden brown. Cool in the pan for 10 minutes, then turn out onto a wire rack to cool.

For the syrup, place the sugar and orange juice in a saucepan and heat gently until the sugar melts. Bring to a boil and simmer for about 5 minutes, until reduced and syrupy.

Spoon the syrup over the cake while it is still warm. Top with the strips of orange zest and serve warm or cold.

Serves 10

scant 1 cup unsalted butter, plus extra for greasing

1 cup superfine sugar

3 extra-large eggs, beaten

finely grated rind of 1 orange

¼ cup poppy seeds

2¼ cups all-purpose flour, plus extra for dusting

2 tsp baking powder

⅔ cup milk

½ cup orange juice

strips of orange zest, to decorate

Syrup

scant ¾ cup superfine sugar

⅔ cup orange juice

GLOSSY FRUIT LOAF

Serves 10

⅓ cup raisins

½ cup plumped dried apricots, coarsely chopped

⅓ cup chopped pitted dates

⅓ cup cold black tea

½ cup butter, plus extra for greasing

generous ½ cup light brown sugar

2 eggs, beaten

1¼ cups self-rising flour, sifted

scant ⅓ cup coarsely chopped candied pineapple

scant ½ cup candied cherries, halved

generous ½ cup coarsely chopped Brazil nuts

Topping

walnut halves

whole Brazil nuts

candied cherries

2 tbsp apricot jelly, strained

Place the raisins, apricots, and dates in a bowl, pour over the tea, and let soak for 8 hours, or overnight.

Preheat the oven to 325°F/160°C. Grease and line a 9 x 5 x 3-inch/23 x 13 x 8-cm loaf pan.

Beat the butter and sugar together until light and fluffy. Gradually beat in the eggs, then fold in the flour alternately with the soaked fruit. Gently stir in the candied pineapple, candied cherries, and chopped Brazil nuts. Spoon the batter into the prepared pan. For the topping, arrange the walnut halves, whole Brazil nuts, and candied cherries over the surface.

Bake in the preheated oven for 1½–1¾ hours, or until a skewer inserted into the center comes out clean. Let cool in the pan for 10 minutes, then turn out and peel off the lining paper. Transfer to a wire rack to cool completely. Warm the apricot jelly in a small saucepan over low heat and brush over the top of the cake.

DATE & WALNUT LOAF

Preheat the oven to 350°F/180°C. Grease an 8 x 4 x 2-inch/20 x 10 x 5-cm loaf pan and line the bottom with parchment paper.

Place the dates, baking soda, and lemon rind in a bowl and add the hot tea. Let soak for 10 minutes, until softened.

Cream together the butter and sugar until light and fluffy, then beat in the egg. Stir in the date mixture.

Fold in the flour using a large metal spoon, then fold in the chopped walnuts. Spoon the mixture into the prepared loaf pan and spread evenly. Top with walnut halves.

Bake in the preheated oven for 35–40 minutes, or until risen, firm, and golden brown. Cool for 10 minutes in the pan, then turn out the loaf and finish cooling on a wire rack.

Serves 8

generous ½ cup chopped pitted dates

½ tsp baking soda

finely grated rind of ½ lemon

scant ½ cup hot tea

3 tbsp butter, plus extra for greasing

⅓ cup light brown sugar

1 egg

generous 1 cup self-rising flour

¼ cup chopped walnuts

walnut halves, to decorate

BLACKBERRY & APPLE LOAF

Serves 10

butter, for greasing

12 oz/350 g baking apples

3 tbsp lemon juice

2½ cups self-rising whole wheat flour

½ tsp baking powder

1 tsp ground cinnamon, plus extra for dusting

¾ cup blackberries, thawed, if frozen

¾ cup light brown sugar

1 egg, beaten

scant 1 cup low-fat plain yogurt

14 white or brown sugar cubes, lightly crushed

Preheat the oven to 375°F/190°C. Grease and line a 9 x 5 x 3-inch/23 x 13 x 8-cm loaf pan.

Peel, core, and finely dice the apples. Place them in a saucepan with the lemon juice, bring to a boil, cover, and simmer for about 10 minutes, until soft and pulpy. Beat well and set aside to cool.

Sift the flour, baking powder, and cinnamon into a bowl, adding any husks that remain in the sifter. Stir in ½ cup of the blackberries and the sugar.

Make a well in the center of the ingredients and add the egg, yogurt, and cooled apple puree. Mix well to incorporate thoroughly.

Spoon the batter into the prepared pan and smooth the top. Sprinkle with the remaining blackberries, pressing them down into the cake batter, and top with the crushed sugar lumps. Bake in the preheated oven for 40–45 minutes. Remove from the oven and set aside in the pan to cool.

Remove the cake from the pan and peel away the lining paper. Serve dusted with cinnamon.

FROSTED CARROT CAKE

Preheat the oven to 350°F/180°C. Grease a 9-inch/23-cm square cake pan and line the bottom with parchment paper.

In a large bowl, beat the oil, brown sugar, and eggs together. Stir in the carrots, golden raisins, walnuts, and orange rind.

Sift together the flour, baking soda, cinnamon, and nutmeg, then stir into the carrot mixture.

Spoon the batter into the prepared cake pan and bake in the preheated oven for 40–45 minutes, until well risen and firm to the touch.

Remove the cake from the oven and set on a wire rack for 5 minutes. Turn out onto the wire rack to cool completely.

For the frosting, combine the cream cheese, confectioners' sugar, and orange juice in a bowl and beat until smooth. Spread over the cake and swirl with a spatula. Decorate with strips of orange zest and serve cut into squares.

Serves 16

¾ cup sunflower oil, plus extra for greasing
¾ cup light brown sugar
3 eggs, beaten
1¼ cups grated carrots
⅔ cup golden raisins
½ cup walnut pieces
grated rind of 1 orange
1½ cups self-rising flour
1 tsp baking soda
1 tsp ground cinnamon
½ tsp grated nutmeg
strips of orange zest, to decorate

Frosting

scant 1 cup cream cheese
scant 1 cup confectioners' sugar
2 tsp orange juice

HUMMINGBIRD CAKE

Serves 10

125 g/4½ oz canned crushed pineapple (in juice)

2¼ cups all-purpose flour

1¼ cups superfine sugar

1 tsp ground cinnamon

1 tsp baking soda

3 eggs, beaten

scant 1 cup sunflower oil, plus extra for greasing

scant 1 cup pecans, coarsely chopped, plus extra to decorate

1 cup mashed ripe bananas (about 3 bananas)

Frosting

¾ cup cream cheese

½ cup unsalted butter

1 tsp vanilla extract

3½ cups confectioners' sugar

Preheat the oven to 350°F/180°C. Lightly grease 3 x 23-cm/ 9-inch round layer cake pans with oil and line the bottoms with parchment paper. Drain the pineapple, reserving 4 tablespoons of the juice. Set aside.

Sift together the flour, superfine sugar, cinnamon, and baking soda into a large bowl. Add the eggs, oil, pecans, bananas, pineapple, and pineapple juice, and stir with a wooden spoon until evenly mixed.

Divide the mixture among the prepared pans, spreading evenly. Bake in the preheated oven for 25–30 minutes, or until golden brown and firm to the touch.

Remove the cakes from the oven and let cool for 10 minutes in the pans before turning out onto wire racks to cool.

For the frosting, beat together the cream cheese, butter, and vanilla extract in a bowl until smooth. Sift in the confectioners' sugar and mix until smooth.

Sandwich the cakes together with half of the frosting, spread the remaining frosting over the top, then sprinkle with chopped pecans to decorate.

RED VELVET CAKE

Preheat the oven to 375°F/190°C. Grease 2 x 9-inch/23-cm layer cake pans and line the bottoms with parchment paper.

Place the butter, water, and cocoa in a small saucepan and heat gently, without boiling, stirring until melted and smooth. Remove from the heat and let cool slightly.

Beat together the eggs, buttermilk, vanilla extract, and food coloring until frothy. Beat in the butter mixture. Sift together the flour, cornstarch, and baking powder, then stir quickly and evenly into the mixture with the superfine sugar.

Divide the batter between the prepared pans and bake in the preheated oven for 25–30 minutes, or until risen and firm to the touch. Cool in the pans for 3–4 minutes, then turn out and finish cooling on a wire rack.

For the frosting, beat together all the ingredients until smooth. Use about half of the frosting to sandwich the cakes together, then spread the remainder over the top, swirling with a metal spatula.

* If you prefer not to use synthetic food coloring, you can replace it with 4 tablespoons of beet juice, but reduce the water quantity to 2 tablespoons.

Serves 12

1 cup unsalted butter, plus extra for greasing

4 tbsp water

½ cup unsweetened cocoa

3 eggs

generous 1 cup buttermilk

2 tsp vanilla extract

2 tbsp red edible food coloring*

2½ cups all-purpose flour

½ cup cornstarch

1½ tsp baking powder

scant 1½ cups superfine sugar

Frosting

generous 1 cup cream cheese

3 tbsp unsalted butter

3 tbsp superfine sugar

1 tsp vanilla extract

COCONUT BARS

Makes 10

generous ½ cup butter, plus extra for greasing

generous 1 cup superfine sugar

2 eggs, beaten

finely grated rind of 1 orange

3 tbsp orange juice

⅔ cup sour cream

1¼ cups self-rising flour

1 cup dry unsweetened coconut

toasted long shred coconut, to decorate

Frosting

1 egg white

1¾ cups confectioners' sugar

1 cup dry unsweetened coconut

about 1 tbsp orange juice

Preheat the oven to 350°F/180°C. Grease a 9-inch/ 23-cm square cake pan and line the bottom with parchment paper.

Cream together the butter and superfine sugar until pale and fluffy, then gradually beat in the eggs. Stir in the orange rind, orange juice, and sour cream. Fold in the flour and dry unsweetened coconut evenly using a metal spoon.

Spoon the batter into the prepared cake pan and level the surface. Bake in the preheated oven for 35–40 minutes, or until risen and firm to the touch.

Let cool for 10 minutes in the pan, then turn out and finish cooling on a wire rack.

For the frosting, lightly beat the egg white just enough to break it up and stir in the confectioners' sugar and dry unsweetened coconut, adding enough orange juice to mix to a thick paste. Spread over the top of the cake, sprinkle with long shred coconut, then let set before slicing into bars.

LEMON DRIZZLE BARS

Preheat the oven to 350°F/180°C. Grease a 7-inch/18-cm square cake pan and line with parchment paper.

Place the eggs, superfine sugar, and margarine in a bowl and beat hard until smooth and fluffy. Stir in the lemon rind, then fold in the flour lightly and evenly. Stir in the milk, mixing evenly, then spoon into the prepared cake pan, smoothing level.

Bake in the preheated oven for 45–50 minutes, or until golden brown and firm to the touch. Remove from the oven and place the pan on a wire rack.

To make the syrup, place the confectioners' sugar and lemon juice in a small saucepan and heat gently, stirring until the sugar dissolves. Do not boil.

Prick the warm cake all over with a skewer and spoon the hot syrup evenly over the top.

Let cool completely in the pan, then turn out the cake, cut into 12 pieces, and dust with a little confectioners' sugar before serving.

Makes 12

2 eggs

generous ¾ cup superfine sugar

⅔ cup soft margarine, plus extra for greasing

finely grated rind of 1 lemon

1½ cups self-rising flour

½ cup milk

Syrup

1¼ cups confectioners' sugar, plus extra for dusting

¼ cup lemon juice

TOFFEE APPLE SQUARES

Makes 9

Brownies

½ cup butter, plus extra
for greasing

¾ cup light brown sugar

2 eggs, beaten

1¾ cups all-purpose flour

1 tsp baking powder

½ tsp baking soda

1½ tsp apple pie spice

2 apples, peeled and coarsely
grated

¾ cup chopped hazelnuts

Toffee apple topping

generous ⅓ cup light
brown sugar

4 tbsp unsalted butter

1 apple, cored and
thinly sliced

Preheat the oven to 350°F/180°C. Grease a 9-inch/23-cm square, shallow cake pan.

For the topping, place the sugar and butter in a small pan and heat gently, stirring, until melted. Pour into the prepared cake pan. Arrange the apple slices on top.

For the brownies, place the butter and sugar in a bowl and beat well until pale and fluffy. Gradually beat in the eggs. Sift in the flour, baking powder, baking soda, and spice and fold into the mixture. Stir in the grated apples and hazelnuts.

Pour into the prepared cake pan and bake in the preheated oven for 35–40 minutes, until firm and golden. Cool in the pan for 10 minutes, then turn out and cut into squares.

CRUNCHY

Temptingly tasty cookies

CHOCOLATE CHIP COOKIES

Preheat the oven to 375°F/190°C. Lightly grease 2 cookie sheets.

Place all of the ingredients in a large mixing bowl and beat until thoroughly combined.

Place tablespoonfuls of the mixture onto the cookie sheets, spacing them well apart to allow for spreading during cooking.

Bake in the preheated oven for 10–12 minutes, or until the cookies are golden brown.

Using a spatula, transfer the cookies to a wire rack to cool completely.

Makes 30

1½ cups all-purpose flour

1 tsp baking powder

½ cup soft margarine, plus extra for greasing

½ cup light brown sugar

¼ cup superfine sugar

½ tsp vanilla extract

1 egg

⅔ cup semisweet chocolate chips

CLASSIC OAT COOKIES

Makes 30

¾ cup butter or margarine, plus extra for greasing

scant 1⅓ cups raw sugar

1 egg

4 tbsp water

1 tsp vanilla extract

4⅓ cups rolled oats

1 cup all-purpose flour

1 tsp salt

½ tsp baking soda

Preheat the oven to 350°F/180°C. Grease a large cookie sheet.

Cream the butter and sugar together in a large mixing bowl. Beat in the egg, water, and vanilla extract until the mixture is smooth.

In a separate bowl, mix the oats, flour, salt, and baking soda. Gradually stir the oat mixture into the creamed mixture until thoroughly combined.

Place tablespoonfuls of the mixture onto the prepared cookie sheet, making sure they are well spaced. Transfer to the preheated oven and bake for 15 minutes, or until the cookies are golden brown.

Remove the cookies from the oven and place on a wire rack to cool before serving.

CHEWY GOLDEN COOKIES

Preheat the oven to 350°F/180°C. Grease a large cookie sheet.

In a large mixing bowl, beat the butter, brown sugar, corn syrup, and egg whites together. Gradually add the oats, flour, salt, and baking powder and mix thoroughly.

Drop 30 rounded tablespoonfuls of the cookie dough onto the cookie sheet. Bake in the preheated oven for 12 minutes, or until the cookies are light brown.

Remove from the oven and let cool on a wire rack. To make the frosting, combine the confectioners' sugar with a little water, drizzle over the cookies, and let set.

Makes 30

¾ cup butter or margarine, plus extra for greasing

scant 1½ cups light brown sugar

1 cup dark corn syrup

3 egg whites

6 cups rolled oats

2 cups all-purpose flour

pinch of salt

1 tsp baking powder

2 tbsp confectioners' sugar

OAT, RAISIN & NUT COOKIES

Makes about 30

scant ½ cup raisins, chopped

½ cup orange juice

1 cup butter, softened

scant ¾ cup superfine sugar

1 egg yolk, lightly beaten

2 tsp vanilla extract

2 cups all-purpose flour

pinch of salt

½ cup rolled oats

½ cup chopped hazelnuts

whole hazelnuts to decorate

Preheat the oven to 375°F/190°C. Line 2 cookie sheets with parchment paper.

Put the raisins in a bowl, add the orange juice, and let soak for 10 minutes.

Put the butter and sugar into a bowl and mix well with a wooden spoon, then beat in the egg yolk and vanilla extract. Sift the flour and salt into the mixture and add the oats and chopped hazelnuts. Drain the raisins, add them to the mixture, and stir until thoroughly combined.

Scoop up tablespoons of the mixture and put them in mounds on the prepared cookie sheets, spaced well apart. Flatten slightly and place a whole hazelnut in the center of each cookie.

Bake in the preheated oven for 12–15 minutes, until golden brown. Let cool on the cookie sheets for 5–10 minutes, then carefully transfer the cookies to wire racks to cool completely.

STICKY GINGER COOKIES

Put the butter and sugar into a bowl and mix well with a wooden spoon, then beat in the egg yolk and ginger syrup. Sift the flour and salt into the mixture, add the preserved ginger and chocolate chips, and stir until thoroughly combined.

Shape the mixture into a log, wrap in plastic wrap, and chill in the refrigerator for 30–60 minutes.

Preheat the oven to 375°F/190°C. Line 2 cookie sheets with parchment paper.

Unwrap the log and cut it into ¼-inch/5-mm slices with a sharp serrated knife. Put them on the prepared cookie sheets, spaced well apart.

Bake in the preheated oven for 12–15 minutes, until golden brown. Let cool on the cookie sheets for 5–10 minutes, then carefully transfer the cookies to wire racks to cool completely.

Makes 20

1 cup butter, softened

scant ¾ cup superfine sugar

1 egg yolk, lightly beaten

¼ cup coarsely chopped preserved ginger, plus 1 tbsp syrup from the jar

2½ cups all-purpose flour

pinch of salt

⅓ cup semisweet chocolate chips

APRICOT & PECAN COOKIES

Makes about 30

1 cup butter, softened

scant ¾ cup superfine sugar

1 egg yolk, lightly beaten

2 tsp vanilla extract

2½ cups all-purpose flour

pinch of salt

grated rind of 1 orange

¼ cup plumped dried apricots, chopped

scant 1 cup finely chopped pecans

Put the butter and sugar into a bowl and mix well with a wooden spoon, then beat in the egg yolk and vanilla extract. Sift the flour and salt into the mixture, add the orange rind and apricots, and stir until thoroughly combined.

Shape the dough into a log. Spread out the pecans in a shallow dish. Roll the log in the pecans until well coated, then wrap in plastic wrap and chill in the refrigerator for 30–60 minutes.

Preheat the oven to 375°F/190°C. Line 2 cookie sheets with parchment paper

Unwrap the dough and cut into ¼-inch/5-mm slices with a sharp serrated knife. Put the slices on the prepared cookie sheets, spaced well apart.

Bake in the preheated oven for 10–12 minutes. Let cool on the cookie sheets for 5–10 minutes, then carefully transfer to wire racks to cool completely.

PEANUT BUTTER COOKIES

Preheat the oven to 350°F/180°C. Grease 3 cookie sheets.

Place the butter and peanut butter in a bowl and beat together. Beat in the superfine sugar and brown sugar, then gradually beat in the egg and vanilla extract.

Sift the flour, baking soda, baking powder, and salt into the bowl and stir in the oats.

Place spoonfuls of the cookie dough onto the cookie sheets, spaced well apart to allow for spreading. Flatten slightly with a fork.

Bake in the preheated oven for 12 minutes, or until lightly browned. Let cool on the cookie sheets for 2 minutes, then transfer to wire racks to cool completely.

Makes 26

½ cup butter, softened, plus extra for greasing

scant ½ cup crunchy peanut butter

generous ½ cup superfine sugar

generous ½ cup light brown sugar

1 egg, beaten

½ tsp vanilla extract

⅔ cup all-purpose flour

½ tsp baking soda

½ tsp baking powder

pinch of salt

1½ cups rolled oats

BANANA & RAISIN COOKIES

Makes about 30

scant ¼ cup raisins

½ cup orange juice or rum

1 cup butter, softened

scant ¾ cup superfine sugar

1 egg yolk, lightly beaten

2½ cups all-purpose flour

pinch of salt

3 oz/85 g dried bananas, finely chopped

Put the raisins into a bowl, pour in the orange juice, and let soak for 30 minutes. Drain the raisins, reserving any remaining orange juice.

Preheat the oven to 375°F/190°C. Line 2 cookie sheets with parchment paper.

Put the butter and sugar into a bowl and mix well with a wooden spoon, then beat in the egg yolk and 2 teaspoons of the reserved orange juice. Sift the flour and salt into the mixture, add the raisins and dried bananas, and stir until thoroughly combined.

Put tablespoons of the mixture into heaps on the prepared cookie sheets, spaced well apart, then flatten them gently. Bake in the preheated oven for 12–15 minutes, until golden. Let cool on the cookie sheets for 5–10 minutes, then carefully transfer to wire racks to cool completely.

GINGERSNAPS

Preheat the oven to 325°F/160°C. Lightly grease several cookie sheets.

Sift together the flour, salt, sugar, ground ginger, and baking soda into a large mixing bowl.

Heat the butter and corn syrup in a saucepan over very low heat until the butter has melted. Let the butter mixture cool slightly, then pour it onto the dry ingredients.

Add the egg and orange rind and mix together thoroughly. Using your hands, carefully shape the dough into 30 even-size balls.

Place the balls on the prepared cookie sheets, spaced well apart, then flatten them slightly with your fingers.

Bake in the preheated oven for 15–20 minutes. Carefully transfer the cookies to a wire rack to cool and become crispy.

Makes 30

2½ cups self-rising flour

pinch of salt

1 cup superfine sugar

1 tbsp ground ginger

1 tsp baking soda

½ cup butter, plus extra for greasing

¼ cup dark corn syrup

1 egg, lightly beaten

1 tsp grated orange rind

WALNUT & COFFEE COOKIES

Makes about 30

2 envelopes instant latte powder

1 tbsp hot water

1 cup butter, softened

scant ¾ cup superfine sugar

1 egg yolk, lightly beaten

2½ cups all-purpose flour

pinch of salt

scant 1 cup finely chopped walnuts

coffee sugar crystals, for sprinkling

Put the latte powder into a bowl and stir in the hot, but not boiling, water to make a paste. Put the butter and sugar into a bowl and mix well with a wooden spoon, then beat in the egg yolk and coffee paste. Sift the flour and salt into the mixture, add the walnuts, and stir until thoroughly combined. Halve the dough, wrap in plastic wrap, and chill in the refrigerator for 30–60 minutes.

Preheat the oven to 375°F/190°C. Line 2 cookie sheets with parchment paper.

Unwrap the dough and roll out between 2 sheets of parchment paper to about ⅛ inch/3 mm thick. Stamp out cookies with a 2½-inch/6-cm round cutter and put them on the prepared cookie sheets, spaced well apart.

Lightly brush the cookies with water, sprinkle with the coffee sugar crystals, and bake in the preheated oven for 10–12 minutes. Let cool on the cookie sheets for 5–10 minutes, then carefully transfer the cookies to wire racks to cool completely.

CITRUS CRESCENTS

Preheat the oven to 400°F/200°C. Lightly grease 2 cookie sheets.

In a mixing bowl, cream together the butter and sugar until light and fluffy, then gradually beat in the egg yolk.

Sift the flour into the creamed mixture and mix until evenly combined. Add the orange rind, lemon rind, and lime rind to the mixture with enough of the orange juice to make a soft dough.

Roll out the dough on a lightly floured counter. Stamp out circles using a 3-inch/7.5-cm cookie cutter. Make crescent shapes by cutting away one quarter of each circle. Reroll the trimmings to make about 25 crescents in total.

Place the crescents onto the prepared cookie sheets. Prick the surface of each crescent with a fork. Lightly beat the egg white in a small bowl and brush it over the cookies.

Bake in the preheated oven for 12–15 minutes. Let the cookies cool on a wire rack before serving.

Makes about 25

⅓ cup butter, softened, plus extra for greasing

⅓ cup superfine sugar

1 egg, separated

1¾ cups all-purpose flour, plus extra for dusting

grated rind of 1 orange

grated rind of 1 lemon

grated rind of 1 lime

2–3 tbsp orange juice

FLOWER GEMS

Makes about 30

1 cup butter, softened

scant ¾ cup superfine sugar

1 egg yolk, lightly beaten

1 tsp lemon juice

2½ cups all-purpose flour

pinch of salt

2 tbsp jasmine tea leaves

orange, pink, blue, and yellow sugar flowers, to decorate

Frosting

1 tbsp lemon juice

1 tbsp water

1¾ cups confectioners' sugar

orange, pink, blue, and yellow food coloring

Put the butter and sugar into a bowl and mix well with a wooden spoon, then beat in the egg yolk and lemon juice. Sift together the flour and salt into the mixture, add the tea leaves, and stir until thoroughly combined. Halve the dough, wrap in plastic wrap, and chill in the refrigerator for 30–60 minutes.

Preheat the oven to 375°F/190°C. Line 2 cookie sheets with parchment paper.

Roll out the dough between 2 sheets of parchment paper to about ⅛ inch/3 mm thick. Stamp out flowers with a 2-inch/5-cm flower-shaped cutter. Put them on the prepared cookie sheets, spaced well apart.

Bake in the preheated oven for 10–12 minutes, until golden brown. Let cool on the cookie sheets for 5–10 minutes, then carefully transfer the cookies to wire racks to cool completely.

For the frosting, mix the lemon juice with the water in a bowl, then gradually stir in enough of the confectioners' sugar to make a mixture with the consistency of thick cream. Divide the frosting among 4 separate bowls and add a drop of different food coloring to each.

With the cookies still on the racks, spread orange frosting on one quarter of the cookies, pink on another quarter, and so on. When the frosting is just beginning to set, put a matching sugar flower in the center of each to decorate. Let set completely.

VANILLA HEARTS

Preheat the oven to 350°F/180°C. Lightly grease a cookie sheet.

Sift the flour into a large bowl. Add the butter and rub it in with your fingertips until the mixture resembles fine breadcrumbs. Stir in the sugar and vanilla extract and mix together to form a firm dough.

Roll out the dough on a lightly floured counter to a thickness of ½ inch/1 cm. Stamp out 12 hearts with a heart-shaped cookie cutter measuring 2 inches/5 cm across. Arrange the hearts on the prepared cookie sheet.

Bake in the preheated oven for 15–20 minutes, or until just colored. Transfer to a wire rack and let cool completely. Dust with a little superfine sugar just before serving.

Makes 12

1½ cups all-purpose flour, plus extra for dusting

scant ¾ cup butter, cut into small pieces, plus extra for greasing

generous 1 cup superfine sugar, plus extra for dusting

1 tsp vanilla extract

JELLY RINGS

Makes about 15

1 cup butter, softened

scant ¾ cup superfine sugar, plus extra for sprinkling

1 egg yolk, lightly beaten

2 tsp vanilla extract

2½ cups all-purpose flour

pinch of salt

1 egg white, lightly beaten

Filling

¼ cup butter, softened

scant 1 cup confectioners' sugar

5 tbsp strawberry jelly or raspberry jelly, warmed

Put the butter and superfine sugar into a bowl and mix well with a wooden spoon, then beat in the egg yolk and vanilla extract. Sift the flour and salt into the mixture and stir until thoroughly combined. Halve the dough, wrap in plastic wrap, and chill in the refrigerator for 30–60 minutes.

Preheat the oven to 375°F/190°C. Line 2 cookie sheets with parchment paper.

Unwrap the dough and roll out between 2 sheets of parchment paper. Stamp out 30 cookies using a 2¾-inch/ 7-cm fluted, round cutter and put half of them on 1 of the prepared cookie sheets, spaced well apart. Using a 1½-inch/4-cm plain, round cutter, stamp out the centers of the remaining cookies and remove. Put the cookie rings on the other cookie sheet, spaced well apart.

Bake in the preheated oven for 7 minutes, then brush the cookie rings with beaten egg white and sprinkle with superfine sugar. Bake for an additional 5–8 minutes, until light golden brown. Let cool on the cookie sheets for 5–10 minutes, then carefully transfer to wire racks to cool completely.

To make the filling, beat the butter and confectioners' sugar together in a bowl until smooth and combined. Spread the buttercream over the whole cookies and top with a little jelly. Place the cookie rings on top and press gently together.

GINGERBREAD PEOPLE

Preheat the oven to 325°F/160°C. Grease 3 large cookie sheets.

Sift the flour, ginger, allspice, and baking soda into a large bowl. Place the butter, corn syrup, and brown sugar in a saucepan over low heat and stir until melted. Pour onto the dry ingredients and add the egg. Mix together to make a dough. The dough will be sticky to start with, but will become firmer as it cools.

Roll out the dough on a lightly floured counter to a thickness of 1/8 inch/3 mm and stamp out gingerbread people shapes. Place on the prepared cookie sheets. Reknead and reroll the trimmings and cut out more shapes. Decorate with currants for eyes and pieces of candied cherry for mouths. Bake in the preheated oven for 15–20 minutes, until firm and lightly browned.

Remove from the oven and let cool on the cookie sheets for a few minutes, then transfer to wire racks to cool completely.

Mix the confectioners' sugar with the water to a thick consistency. Place the frosting in a small pastry bag fitted with a plain tip and use to pipe buttons or bows onto the cooled cookies.

Makes 20

3½ cups all-purpose flour, plus extra for dusting

2 tsp ground ginger

1 tsp ground allspice

2 tsp baking soda

½ cup butter, plus extra for greasing

generous ⅓ cup dark corn syrup

generous ½ cup light brown sugar

1 egg, beaten

To decorate

currants

candied cherries

generous ¾ cup confectioners' sugar

3–4 tsp water

CHECKERBOARD COOKIES

Makes about 20

1 cup butter, softened

scant ¾ cup superfine sugar

1 egg yolk, lightly beaten

2 tsp vanilla extract

2½ cups all-purpose flour

pinch of salt

1 tsp ground ginger

1 tbsp finely grated orange rind

1 tbsp unsweetened cocoa, sifted

1 egg white, lightly beaten

Put the butter and sugar into a bowl and mix well with a wooden spoon, then beat in the egg yolk and vanilla extract. Sift the flour and salt into the mixture and stir until thoroughly combined.

Divide the dough in half. Add the ginger and orange rind to one half and mix well. Shape the dough into a log 6 inches/15 cm long. Flatten the sides and top to square off the log to 2 inches/5 cm high. Wrap in plastic wrap and chill in the refrigerator for 30–60 minutes. Add the cocoa to the other half of the dough and mix well. Shape into a flattened log exactly the same size as the first one, wrap in plastic wrap, and chill in the refrigerator for 30–60 minutes.

Unwrap the dough and cut each flattened log lengthwise into 3 slices. Cut each slice lengthwise into 3 strips. Brush the strips with egg white and stack them in 3s, alternating the colors, so they are the same shape as the original logs. Wrap in plastic wrap and chill in the refrigerator for 30–60 minutes.

Preheat the oven to 375°F/190°C. Line 2 cookie sheets with parchment paper.

Unwrap the logs and cut into slices with a sharp serrated knife. Put the cookies on the prepared cookie sheets, spaced well apart. Bake in the preheated oven for 12–15 minutes, until firm. Let cool on the cookie sheets for 5–10 minutes, then carefully transfer to wire racks to cool completely.

WALNUT & FIG PINWHEELS

Put the butter and scant ¾ cup of the sugar into a bowl and mix well with a wooden spoon, then beat in the egg yolk. Sift the flour and salt into the mixture, add the walnuts, and stir until thoroughly combined. Shape the dough into a ball, wrap in plastic wrap, and chill for 30–60 minutes.

Meanwhile, put the remaining sugar into a saucepan and stir in the water, then add the figs, mint tea, and chopped mint. Bring to a boil, stirring constantly, until the sugar has dissolved, then lower the heat, and simmer gently, stirring occasionally, for 5 minutes. Remove the saucepan from the heat and let cool.

Unwrap the dough and roll out between 2 sheets of parchment paper into a 12-inch/30-cm square. Spread the fig filling evenly over the dough, then roll up like a jelly roll. Wrap in plastic wrap and chill in the refrigerator for 30 minutes.

Preheat the oven to 375°F/190°C. Line 2 cookie sheets with parchment paper.

Unwrap the roll and cut into thin slices with a sharp serrated knife. Put the slices on the prepared cookie sheets, spaced well apart. Bake in the preheated oven for 10–15 minutes, until golden brown. Let cool on the cookie sheets for 5–10 minutes, then transfer to wire racks to cool completely.

Makes about 30

1 cup butter, softened
1 cup superfine sugar
1 egg yolk, lightly beaten
2 cups all-purpose flour
pinch of salt
½ cup ground walnuts
½ cup water
1⅔ cups dried figs, finely chopped
5 tbsp freshly brewed mint tea
2 tsp finely chopped fresh mint

FROSTED CHERRY RINGS

Makes about 18

½ cup unsalted butter, plus extra for greasing

scant ½ cup superfine sugar

1 egg yolk

finely grated rind of ½ lemon

1¾ cups all-purpose flour, plus extra for dusting

¼ cup candied cherries, finely chopped

Frosting

¾ cup confectioners' sugar

1½ tbsp lemon juice

Preheat the oven to 400°F/200°C. Lightly grease 2 cookie sheets.

Cream together the butter and superfine sugar until pale and fluffy. Beat in the egg yolk and lemon rind. Sift in the flour, stir, then add the candied cherries, mixing with your hands to a soft dough.

Roll out the dough on a lightly floured counter to about ¼ inch/5 mm thick. Stamp out circles with a 3¼-inch/8-cm round cutter. Cut out the center of each with a 1-inch/2.5-cm round cutter and place the rings on the prepared cookie sheets. Reroll any trimmings and cut out more cookies.

Bake in the preheated oven for 12–15 minutes, until firm and golden brown. Let cool on the cookie sheets for 2 minutes, then transfer to a wire rack to cool completely.

Mix the confectioners' sugar to a smooth paste with the lemon juice. Drizzle over the cookies and let set.

153

CAPPUCCINO COOKIES

Empty the cappuccino envelopes into a small bowl and stir in the hot water to make a paste.

Put the butter and sugar into a bowl and mix well with a wooden spoon, then beat in the egg yolk and cappuccino paste. Sift the flour and salt into the mixture and stir until thoroughly combined. Halve the dough, wrap in plastic wrap, and chill in the refrigerator for 30–60 minutes.

Preheat the oven to 375°F/190°C. Line 2 cookie sheets with parchment paper.

Unwrap the dough and roll out between 2 sheets of parchment paper. Stamp out cookies with a 2½-inch/6-cm round cutter and put them on the prepared cookie sheets, spaced well apart.

Bake in the preheated oven for 10–12 minutes, until golden brown. Let cool on the cookie sheets for 5–10 minutes, then using a metal spatula, carefully transfer to wire racks to cool completely.

When the cookies are cool, place the wire racks over a sheet of parchment paper. Put the chocolate into a heatproof bowl set over a saucepan of gently simmering water until melted. Remove the bowl from the heat and let cool, then spoon the chocolate over the cookies. Gently tap the wire racks to level the surface and let set. Dust with cocoa before serving.

Makes about 30
2 envelopes instant cappuccino powder

1 tbsp hot water

1 cup butter, softened

scant ¾ cup superfine sugar

1 egg yolk, lightly beaten

2½ cups all-purpose flour

pinch of salt

6 oz/175 g white chocolate, broken into pieces

unsweetened cocoa, for dusting

CRANBERRY & COCONUT COOKIES

Makes about 30

1 cup butter, softened

scant ¾ cup superfine sugar

1 egg yolk, lightly beaten

2 tsp vanilla extract

2½ cups all-purpose flour

pinch of salt

½ cup unsweetened dried coconut

½ cup dried cranberries

Preheat the oven to 375°F/190°C. Line 2 cookie sheets with parchment paper.

Put the butter and sugar into a bowl and mix well with a wooden spoon, then beat in the egg yolk and vanilla extract. Sift the flour and salt into the mixture, add the coconut and cranberries, and stir until thoroughly combined.

Scoop up tablespoons of the dough and place in mounds on the prepared cookie sheets, spaced well apart.

Bake in the preheated oven for 12–15 minutes, until golden brown. Let cool on the cookie sheets for 5–10 minutes, then carefully transfer to wire racks to cool completely.

CRUNCHY NUT & HONEY SANDWICH COOKIES

Preheat the oven to 375°F/190°C. Line 2 cookie sheets with parchment paper.

Put 1 cup of the butter and the superfine sugar into a bowl and mix well with a wooden spoon, then beat in the egg yolk and vanilla extract. Sift the flour and salt into the mixture and stir until thoroughly combined.

Scoop up tablespoons of the dough and roll into balls. Put half of them on a prepared cookie sheet, spaced well apart, and flatten gently. Spread out the nuts in a shallow dish and dip one side of the remaining dough balls into them, then place on the other cookie sheet, nut-side uppermost, and flatten gently.

Bake in the preheated oven for 10–15 minutes, until light golden brown. Let cool on the cookie sheets for 5–10 minutes, then carefully transfer to wire racks to cool completely.

Beat the remaining butter with the confectioners' sugar and honey until creamy and thoroughly mixed. Spread the honey mixture over the plain cookies and top with the nut-coated cookies.

Makes about 30

1⅓ cups butter, softened

scant ¾ cup superfine sugar

1 egg yolk, lightly beaten

2 tsp vanilla extract

2½ cups all-purpose flour

pinch of salt

⅓ cup macadamia nuts, cashew nuts, or pine nuts, chopped

¾ cup confectioners' sugar

⅓ cup set honey

SNICKERDOODLES

Makes about 40

1 cup butter, softened

scant ¾ cup superfine sugar

2 extra-large eggs, lightly beaten

1 tsp vanilla extract

3½ cups all-purpose flour

1 tsp baking soda

½ tsp freshly grated nutmeg

pinch of salt

½ cup finely chopped pecans

Cinnamon coating

1 tbsp superfine sugar

2 tsp ground cinnamon

Put the butter and sugar into a bowl and mix well with a wooden spoon, then beat in the eggs and vanilla extract. Sift the flour, baking soda, nutmeg, and salt into the mixture, add the pecans, and stir until thoroughly combined. Shape the dough into a ball, wrap in plastic wrap, and chill in the refrigerator for 30–60 minutes.

Preheat the oven to 375°F/190°C. Line 2 cookie sheets with parchment paper.

For the coating, mix together the superfine sugar and cinnamon in a shallow dish. Scoop up tablespoons of the cookie dough and roll into balls. Roll each ball in the cinnamon mixture to coat and put on the prepared cookie sheets, spaced well apart.

Bake in the preheated oven for 10–12 minutes, until golden brown. Let cool on the cookie sheets for 5–10 minutes, then carefully transfer to wire racks to cool completely.

VIENNESE FINGERS

Preheat the oven to 325°F/160°C. Lightly grease 2 cookie sheets.

Place the butter, sugar, and vanilla extract in a bowl and cream together until pale and fluffy. Stir in the flour, mixing evenly to a fairly stiff dough.

Place the mixture in a pastry bag fitted with a large star tip and pipe about 16 bars, each 2½ inches/ 6 cm long, onto the prepared cookie sheets.

Bake in the preheated oven for 10–15 minutes, until pale golden. Let cool for 2–3 minutes on the cookie sheets, then carefully transfer to a wire rack to cool completely.

Place the chocolate in a small heatproof bowl set over a saucepan of gently simmering water until melted. Remove from the heat. Dip the ends of each cookie into the chocolate to coat, then place on a sheet of parchment paper and let set.

Makes about 16

scant ½ cup unsalted butter, plus extra for greasing

2 tbsp superfine sugar

½ tsp vanilla extract

scant 1 cup self-rising flour

3½ oz/100 g semisweet chocolate, broken into pieces

ALMOND MACAROONS

Makes 12–14

1 egg white

¾ cup ground almonds

scant ½ cup superfine sugar, plus extra for rolling

½ tsp almond extract

6–7 blanched almonds, split in half

Preheat the oven to 350°F/180°C. Line 2 cookie sheets with parchment paper.

Beat the egg white with a fork until frothy, then stir in the ground almonds, sugar, and almond extract, mixing to form a sticky dough.

Using lightly sugared hands, roll the dough into small balls and place on the prepared cookie sheets. Press an almond half into the center of each.

Bake in the preheated oven for 15–20 minutes, or until pale golden. Lift onto a wire rack to cool.

LEBKUCHEN

Preheat the oven to 350°F/180°C. Line several cookie sheets with parchment paper.

Put the eggs and sugar in a heatproof bowl set over a saucepan of gently simmering water. Beat until thick and foamy. Remove the bowl from the heat and continue to beat for 2 minutes.

Sift the flour, cocoa, cinnamon, cardamom, cloves, and nutmeg into the bowl and stir in with the ground almonds and mixed peel. Drop generous teaspoonfuls of the cookie dough onto the prepared cookie sheets, spreading them gently into smooth mounds.

Bake in the preheated oven for 15–20 minutes, until light brown and slightly soft to the touch. Cool on the cookie sheets for 10 minutes, then transfer to wire racks to cool completely.

Put the semisweet and white chocolate in 2 separate heatproof bowls set over 2 saucepans of gently simmering water until melted. Dip half the cookies in the melted semisweet chocolate and half in the white chocolate. Sprinkle with sugar crystals and let set.

Makes 60

3 eggs

1 cup superfine sugar

½ cup all-purpose flour

2 tsp unsweetened cocoa

1 tsp ground cinnamon

½ tsp ground cardamom

¼ tsp ground cloves

¼ tsp ground nutmeg

generous 1 cup ground almonds

scant ⅓ cup chopped mixed peel

To decorate

4 oz/115 g semisweet chocolate

4 oz/115 g white chocolate

sugar crystals

ALMOND BISCOTTI

Makes 20–24

1¾ cups all-purpose flour, plus extra for dusting

1 tsp baking powder

pinch of salt

¾ cup superfine sugar

2 eggs, beaten

finely grated rind of 1 orange

½ cup whole blanched almonds, lightly toasted

Preheat the oven to 350°F/180°C. Lightly dust a cookie sheet with flour.

Sift the flour, baking powder, and salt into a bowl. Add the sugar, eggs, and orange rind and mix to form a dough. Knead in the almonds.

Roll out the dough into a ball, cut in half, and roll out each portion into a log about 1½ inches/4 cm in diameter. Place on the prepared cookie sheet and bake in the preheated oven for 10 minutes. Remove from the oven and let cool for 5 minutes.

Using a serrated knife, cut the logs into ½ inch/1 cm thick diagonal slices. Arrange the slices on the cookie sheet and return to the oven for 15 minutes, or until slightly golden. Transfer to a wire rack to cool and crisp.

GOOEY

Dreamy desserts to indulge

APPLE PIE

To make the pie dough, sift the flour and salt into a large bowl. Add the butter and lard and rub in with your fingertips until the mixture resembles fine breadcrumbs. Add the water and gather the mixture together into a dough. Wrap the dough and let chill in the refrigerator for 30 minutes.

Preheat the oven to 425°F/220°C. Roll out almost two thirds of the pie dough thinly and use to line a deep 9-inch/23-cm pie plate or pie pan.

Mix the apples with the sugar and spice and pack into the pastry shell. Add the water if needed, particularly if the apples are a dry variety.

Roll out the remaining pie dough to form a lid. Dampen the edges of the pie rim with water and position the lid, pressing the edges firmly together. Trim and crimp the edges.

Use the trimmings to cut out leaves or other shapes to decorate the top of the pie. Dampen and attach. Glaze the top of the pie with beaten egg or milk, make 1–2 slits in the top, and place the pie on a baking sheet.

Bake in the preheated oven for 20 minutes, then reduce the oven temperature to 350°F/180°C and bake for an additional 30 minutes, or until the pastry is golden brown. Serve hot or cold, sprinkled with sugar.

Serves 6

Pie dough
2½ cups all-purpose flour

pinch of salt

6 tbsp butter or margarine, cut into small pieces

6 tbsp lard or vegetable shortening, cut into small pieces

about 6 tbsp cold water

beaten egg or milk, for glazing

Filling
1 lb 10 oz–2 lb 4 oz/750 g–1 kg baking apples, peeled, cored, and sliced

scant ⅔ cup brown or superfine sugar, plus extra for sprinkling

½–1 tsp ground cinnamon, allspice, or ground ginger

1–2 tbsp water (optional)

LATTICED CHERRY PIE

Serves 8

Pie dough

1 cup all-purpose flour, plus extra for dusting

¼ tsp baking powder

½ tsp allspice

½ tsp salt

¼ cup superfine sugar

4 tbsp cold unsalted butter, diced, plus extra for greasing

1 egg, beaten, plus extra for glazing

Filling

2 lb/900 g pitted fresh cherries or drained canned cherries

½ cup superfine sugar

½ tsp almond extract

2 tsp cherry brandy

¼ tsp allspice

2 tbsp cornstarch

2 tbsp water

2 tbsp unsalted butter, diced

To make the pie dough, sift the flour and baking powder into a large bowl. Stir in the allspice, salt, and sugar. Rub in the butter with your fingertips until the mixture resembles fine breadcrumbs. Add the beaten egg and mix to a firm dough. Cut the dough in half and roll each half into a ball. Wrap in plastic wrap and chill for 30 minutes.

Preheat the oven to 425°F/220°C. Grease a 9-inch/23-cm round tart pan. Roll out the pie dough into 2 x 12-inch/30-cm circles. Use 1 to line the tart pan, trimming the edges to leave an overhang of ½ inch/1 cm.

To make the filling, put half of the cherries and the sugar in a large saucepan. Bring to a simmer over low heat, stirring, for 5 minutes, or until the sugar has dissolved. Stir in the almond extract, brandy, and allspice. In a separate bowl, mix the cornstarch and water to form a paste. Remove the saucepan from the heat, stir in the cornstarch paste, then return to the heat and stir continuously until the mixture boils and thickens. Let cool a little. Stir in the remaining cherries, pour into the pastry shell, then dot with the butter.

Cut the remaining dough circle into long strips about ½ inch/1 cm wide. Place half the strips evenly across the top of the filling in the same direction. Now lay six strips crosswise on top, folding back every other strip each time you add another crosswise strip to form a lattice. Trim off the ends and seal the edges with water. Use your fingers to crimp around the rim, then brush the top with beaten egg to glaze. Cover with foil, then bake in the preheated oven for 30 minutes. Discard the foil, then bake for an additional 15 minutes, or until golden.

175

LEMON MERINGUE PIE

To make the pie dough, sift the flour into a large bowl. Add the butter and rub it in with your fingertips until the mixture resembles breadcrumbs. Mix in the remaining ingredients. Knead briefly on a lightly floured counter. Let the dough rest for 30 minutes.

Preheat the oven to 350°F/180°C. Grease an 8-inch/20-cm round tart pan.

Roll out the dough to a thickness of ¼ inch/5 mm and use to line the prepared pan. Prick with a fork, then line with parchment paper and fill with dried beans. Bake in the preheated oven for 15 minutes. Remove from the oven, then remove the paper and beans and reduce the oven temperature to 300°F/150°C.

To make the filling, mix the cornstarch with a little of the water to form a paste. Pour the remaining water into a pan. Stir in the lemon juice and rind and the cornstarch paste. Bring to a boil, stirring, and cook for 2 minutes. Remove from the heat, let cool slightly, then stir in 5 tablespoons of the superfine sugar and the egg yolks and pour into the pastry shell. Beat the egg whites in a separate bowl until stiff. Gradually beat in the remaining sugar and spread over the pie.

Bake in the oven for 40 minutes, or until the meringue is light brown. Serve.

Serves 6

Pie dough

1½ cups all-purpose flour, plus extra for dusting

¾ cup butter, diced, plus extra for greasing

scant ½ cup confectioners' sugar, sifted

finely grated rind of 1 lemon

1 egg yolk, beaten

3 tbsp milk

Filling

3 tbsp cornstarch

1¼ cups cold water

juice and grated rind of 2 lemons

¾ cup superfine sugar

2 eggs, separated

light cream, to serve

STRAWBERRY CHEESECAKE

Serves 8

Crumb crust

4 tbsp unsalted butter

2⅓ cups crushed graham crackers

½ cup chopped walnuts

Filling

2 cups mascarpone cheese

2 eggs, beaten

3 tbsp superfine sugar

9 oz/250 g white chocolate, broken into pieces

10½ oz/300 g strawberries, hulled and quartered

Topping

¾ cup mascarpone cheese

1 oz/25 g white chocolate shavings

4 strawberries, halved

Preheat the oven to 300°F/150°C.

Melt the butter in a saucepan over low heat and stir in the crushed crackers and the walnuts. Spoon into a 9-inch/23-cm round, springform cake pan and press evenly over the bottom with the back of a spoon. Set aside.

To make the filling, beat the mascarpone cheese in a bowl until smooth, then beat in the eggs and sugar. Melt the white chocolate in a heatproof bowl set over a saucepan of gently simmering water, stirring until smooth. Remove from the heat and let cool slightly, then stir into the cheese mixture. Stir in the strawberries.

Spoon the mixture into the cake pan, spread out evenly, and smooth the surface. Bake in the preheated oven for 1 hour, or until the filling is just firm. Turn off the oven and let the cheesecake cool inside with the door slightly ajar until completely cold. Transfer to a serving plate.

For the topping, spread the mascarpone cheese on top. Decorate with the chocolate shavings and strawberry halves.

WHITE TRUFFLE CAKE

Preheat the oven to 350°F/180°C. Grease an 8-inch/20-cm round, springform cake pan and line the bottom with parchment paper

Melt the chocolate in a heatproof bowl set over a saucepan of gently simmering water. Let cool slightly.

Using an electric mixer, beat the eggs and sugar together in a large bowl until thick and pale—the mixture should leave a trail when the beaters are lifted. Sift the flour and gently fold into the egg mixture with a metal spoon. Add the melted chocolate and fold in.

Pour the batter into the prepared pan and bake in the preheated oven for 25 minutes, or until springy to the touch. Let cool slightly in the pan, then transfer to a wire rack and let cool completely. Return the cold cake to the pan.

To make the topping, put the cream in a saucepan and bring to a boil, stirring continuously. Let cool slightly, then add the chocolate and stir until melted and combined. Remove from the heat and set aside until almost cool, stirring, then mix in the mascarpone cheese. Pour on top of the cake. Let chill in the refrigerator for 2 hours.

Decorate with the chocolate shavings before serving.

Serves 12

butter, for greasing

1¾ oz/50 g white chocolate

2 eggs

¼ cup superfine sugar

½ cup all-purpose flour

Topping

1¼ cups heavy cream

12 oz/350 g white chocolate, broken into pieces

generous 1 cup mascarpone cheese

1¾ oz/50 g white chocolate shavings

SYRUP TART

Serves 8

9 oz/250 g prepared unsweetened pie dough

all-purpose flour, for dusting

1½ cups dark corn syrup

2¼ cups fresh white breadcrumbs

½ cup heavy cream

finely grated rind of ½ lemon or orange

2 tbsp lemon juice or orange juice

whipped cream, to serve

Roll out the pie dough on a lightly floured counter and use to line an 8-inch/20-cm round, loose-bottom tart pan, reserving the dough trimmings. Prick the bottom of the pie dough with a fork and chill in the refrigerator. Reroll the reserved dough trimmings and cut out small shapes, such as leaves, stars, or hearts, to decorate the top of the tart.

Preheat the oven to 375°F/190°C.

Mix the corn syrup, breadcrumbs, heavy cream, lemon rind, and lemon juice together in a small bowl. Pour the mixture into the pastry shell and decorate the top of the tart with the dough shapes.

Bake in the preheated oven for 35–40 minutes, or until the filling is just set.

Remove from the oven and let the tart cool slightly in the pan before turning out and serving with whipped cream.

BANANA & TOFFEE PIE

Place the unopened cans of condensed milk in a large pan and add enough water to cover them. Bring to a boil, then reduce the heat and let simmer for 2 hours, adding extra water as needed to keep the cans covered. Carefully lift out the hot cans from the pan and let cool.

Preheat the oven to 350°F/180°C. Grease a 9-inch/23-cm round tart pan.

For the crumb crust, put the butter in a bowl and add the crushed graham crackers and ground nuts. Mix together well, then press the mixture evenly over the bottom and sides of the tart pan. Bake in the preheated oven for 10–12 minutes, then remove from the oven and let cool.

Peel and slice the bananas and place in a bowl. Squeeze over the juice from the lemon, add the vanilla extract, and mix together. Spread the banana mixture over the crumb crust, then spoon the contents of the cooled cans of condensed milk over the bananas. Sprinkle over two thirds of the chocolate, then top with a layer of whipped cream. Sprinkle over the remaining grated chocolate and serve the pie at room temperature.

Serves 4–6

Filling

2 x 14-oz/400-g cans sweetened condensed milk

4 ripe bananas

juice of ½ lemon

1 tsp vanilla extract

2¾ oz/75 g semisweet chocolate, grated

2 cups heavy cream, whipped

Crumb crust

6 tbsp butter, melted, plus extra for greasing

5½ oz/150 g graham crackers, crushed

scant ⅓ cup shelled almonds, toasted and ground

scant ⅓ cup shelled hazelnuts, toasted and ground

PECAN PIE

Serves 8

Pie dough

1¾ cups all-purpose flour, plus extra for dusting

½ cup butter

2 tbsp superfine sugar

Filling

5 tbsp butter

scant ½ cup light brown sugar

⅔ cup dark corn syrup

2 extra-large eggs, beaten

1 tsp vanilla extract

1 cup pecans

For the pie dough, place the flour in a bowl and rub in the butter using your fingertips until it resembles fine breadcrumbs. Stir in the superfine sugar and add enough cold water to mix to a firm dough. Wrap in plastic wrap and chill for 15 minutes, until firm enough to roll out.

Preheat the oven to 400°F/200°C. Roll out the dough on a lightly floured counter and use to line a 9-inch/23-cm round, loose-bottom tart pan. Prick the bottom with a fork. Chill for 15 minutes.

Place the tart pan on a cookie sheet, line with a sheet of parchment paper, and fill with dried beans. Bake in the preheated oven for 10 minutes. Remove the paper and beans and bake for an additional 5 minutes. Reduce the oven temperature to 350°F/180°C.

For the filling, place the butter, brown sugar, and corn syrup in a saucepan and heat gently until melted. Remove from the heat and quickly beat in the eggs and vanilla extract.

Coarsely chop the pecans and stir into the mixture. Pour into the tart shell and bake for 35–40 minutes, until the filling is just set. Serve warm or cold.

SWEET PUMPKIN PIE

Preheat the oven to 375°F/190°C. Put the pumpkin halves, face down, in a roasting pan and cover with foil. Bake in the preheated oven for 1½ hours. Scoop out the flesh and puree in a food processor. Drain off any excess liquid.

Grease a 9-inch/23-cm round tart pan. Sift the flour and baking powder into a bowl. Stir in ½ teaspoon of the cinnamon, ¼ teaspoon of the nutmeg, ¼ teaspoon of the cloves, ½ teaspoon of the salt, and all the superfine sugar. Rub in the butter with your fingertips until the mixture resembles breadcrumbs. Lightly beat 1 of the eggs, then add to the bowl. Mix together to form a dough, then shape into a ball. Roll out on a lightly floured counter and use to line the pan. Chill for 30 minutes.

Preheat the oven to 425°F/220°C. Put the pumpkin in a bowl, then stir in the condensed milk and the remaining eggs. Add the remaining spices and salt, then stir in the vanilla extract and raw sugar. Pour into the pastry shell and bake in the preheated oven for 15 minutes.

Meanwhile, make the topping. Mix the flour, raw sugar, and cinnamon in a bowl, rub in the butter, then stir in the nuts. Remove the pie from the oven and reduce the heat to 350°F/180°C. Sprinkle over the topping, then bake for an additional 35 minutes. Serve warm.

Serves 6

4 lb/1.8 kg sweet pumpkin, halved and seeded

1 cup all-purpose flour, plus extra for dusting

¼ tsp baking powder

1½ tsp ground cinnamon

¾ tsp ground nutmeg

¾ tsp ground cloves

1 tsp salt

½ cup superfine sugar

4 tbsp cold unsalted butter, diced, plus extra for greasing

3 eggs

1¾ cups canned sweetened condensed milk

½ tsp vanilla extract

1 tbsp raw sugar

Streusel topping

2 tbsp all-purpose flour

4 tbsp raw sugar

1 tsp ground cinnamon

2 tbsp cold unsalted butter, cut into small pieces

generous ⅔ cup chopped pecans

generous ⅔ cup chopped walnuts

SWEET POTATO PIE

Serves 8

Pie dough

1¼ cups all-purpose flour, plus extra for dusting

½ tsp salt

¼ tsp superfine sugar

1½ tbsp butter, diced

3 tbsp shortening, diced

2–2½ tbsp cold water

Filling

1 lb 2 oz/500 g orange-fleshed sweet potatoes, peeled

3 extra-large eggs, beaten

½ cup light brown sugar

1½ cups canned condensed milk

3 tbsp butter, melted

2 tsp vanilla extract

1 tsp ground cinnamon

1 tsp ground nutmeg

½ tsp salt

To make the pie dough, sift the flour, salt, and superfine sugar into a bowl. Add the butter and shortening to the bowl and rub in with your fingertips until the mixture resembles fine breadcrumbs. Sprinkle over 2 tablespoons of the water and mix with a fork to make a soft dough. If the dough is too dry, sprinkle over the remaining water. Wrap in plastic wrap and chill in the refrigerator for 1 hour.

Meanwhile, bring a large saucepan of water to a boil over high heat. Add the sweet potatoes and cook for 15 minutes. Drain, then cool under cold running water. When cool, cut each into 8 wedges. Place the potatoes in a bowl and beat in the eggs and brown sugar until very smooth. Beat in the remaining ingredients, then set aside.

Preheat the oven to 425°F/220°C. Roll out the pie dough on a lightly floured counter into a thin 11-inch/28-cm circle and use to line a 9-inch/23-cm round tart pan, about 1½ inches/4 cm deep. Trim off the excess dough and press a floured fork around the edge. Prick the bottom of the pastry shell all over with the fork. Line with parchment paper and fill with dried beans. Bake in the preheated oven for 12 minutes, until lightly golden. Remove from the oven and take out the paper and beans.

Pour the filling into the pastry shell and return to the oven for an additional 10 minutes. Reduce the oven temperature to 325°F/160°C and bake for an additional 35 minutes, or until a knife inserted into the center comes out clean. Let cool on a wire rack. Serve warm or at room temperature.

STRAWBERRY TARTLETS

To make the pie dough, sift the flour and confectioners' sugar into a bowl. Chop the butter into small pieces and add to the flour mixture with the egg yolk, mixing with your fingertips and adding a little water, if necessary, to mix to a soft dough. Cover and chill for 15 minutes.

Preheat the oven to 400°F/200°C. Roll out the dough and use to line 4 x 3½-inch/9-cm round tartlet pans. Prick the bottoms with a fork, line with parchment paper, and fill with dried beans, then bake in the preheated oven for 10 minutes. Remove the paper and beans and bake for an additional 5 minutes, until golden. Let cool.

For the filling, place the vanilla bean in a saucepan with the milk and set over low heat to steep, without boiling, for 10 minutes. Beat the egg yolks, superfine sugar, flour, and cornstarch together in a mixing bowl until smooth. Strain the milk into the bowl and beat until smooth. Pour the mixture back into the pan and stir over medium heat until boiling. Cook, stirring continuously, for about 2 minutes, until thickened and smooth. Remove from the heat and fold in the whipped cream. Spoon the mixture into the pie shells.

Let cool and set. When the filling has set slightly, top with strawberries, then spoon over a little grape jelly to glaze.

Serves 8

Pie dough
generous 1 cup all-purpose flour

2 tbsp confectioners' sugar

5 tbsp unsalted butter, softened

1 egg yolk

1–2 tbsp water

Filling
1 vanilla bean, split

scant 1 cup milk

2 egg yolks

3 tbsp superfine sugar

1 tbsp all-purpose flour

1 tbsp cornstarch

½ cup heavy cream, whipped

3 cups strawberries, hulled and halved

4 tbsp grape jelly, warmed

BAKLAVA

Makes 25

2 cups walnut halves

1¾ cups shelled pistachios

¾ cup blanched almonds

4 tbsp pine nuts, chopped finely

finely grated rind of 2 large oranges

6 tbsp sesame seeds

1 tbsp sugar

½ tsp ground cinnamon

½ tsp allspice

23 sheets filo dough, thawed if frozen

1 cup butter, melted, plus extra for greasing

Syrup

3 cups superfine sugar

2 cups water

5 tbsp honey

3 cloves

2 large strips of lemon zest

To make the filling, put the walnuts, pistachios, almonds, and pine nuts in a food processor and process gently, until finely chopped but not ground. Transfer the chopped nuts to a bowl and stir in the orange rind, sesame seeds, sugar, cinnamon, and allspice.

Grease a 10-inch/25-cm square ovenproof dish, about 2 inches/5 cm deep. Preheat the oven to 325°F/160°C. Stack the filo sheets and cut to size, using a ruler. Keep the sheets covered with a damp dish towel. Place a sheet of filo on the bottom of the dish and brush with melted butter. Top with 7 more sheets, brushing with butter between each layer.

Sprinkle with 1 cup of the filling. Top with 3 sheets of filo, brushing each one with butter. Continue layering with 3 sheets at a time until you have used up all the filo and filling, ending with a top layer of 3 sheets of filo. Brush with butter.

Using a sharp knife, cut the baklava into 2-inch/5-cm squares or diamonds. Brush again with butter. Bake in the preheated oven for 1 hour.

Meanwhile, put all the syrup ingredients in a pan, stirring to dissolve the sugar. Bring to a boil, then simmer for 15 minutes, without stirring, until a thin syrup forms. Let cool.

Remove the baklava from the oven and pour the syrup over the top. Let set in the dish, then remove the squares to serve.

STICKY DATE CAKE

Preheat the oven to 350°F/180°C. Grease an 8-inch/20-cm round cake pan.

To make the sponge, put the golden raisins, dates, and baking soda into a heatproof bowl. Cover with boiling water and set aside to soak. Put the butter in a separate bowl, add the sugar, and mix well. Beat in the eggs, then fold in the flour. Drain the soaked golden raisins and dates, add to the bowl, and mix.

Spoon the mixture evenly into the prepared pan. Bake in the preheated oven for 35–40 minutes, or until a skewer inserted into the center comes out clean.

About 5 minutes before the end of the cooking time, make the sauce. Melt the butter in a pan over medium heat. Stir in the cream and sugar and bring to a boil, stirring constantly. Lower the heat and simmer for 5 minutes.

Turn out the sponge onto a serving plate and pour over the sauce. Serve immediately.

Serves 6–8

Sponge
scant ½ cup golden raisins

generous ¾ cup pitted dates, chopped

1 tsp baking soda

2 tbsp butter, plus extra for greasing

1 cup light brown sugar

2 eggs

scant 1½ cups self-rising flour, sifted

Sauce
2 tbsp butter

¾ cup heavy cream

1 cup light brown sugar

PEAR & TOFFEE CRUMBLE

Serves 4

Crumble topping

¾ cup self-rising flour

½ cup unsalted butter, diced

5 tbsp raw sugar

2 tbsp finely chopped hazelnuts

Filling

3 tbsp dark corn syrup

3 tbsp raw sugar

2 tbsp unsalted butter

2 tbsp light cream

½ tsp vanilla extract

4 large pears

vanilla ice cream, to serve

Preheat the oven to 400°F/200°C.

To make the crumble topping, put the flour in a large heatproof bowl and rub in the butter with your fingertips, until the mixture resembles fine breadcrumbs. Stir in 4 tablespoons of the sugar and the chopped hazelnuts, then cook in the preheated oven for 5–10 minutes, until heated through.

To make the toffee filling, put the corn syrup into a saucepan over low heat. Add the sugar, half the butter, the cream and vanilla extract, and bring gently to a boil. Simmer for 3 minutes, stirring constantly, then remove from the heat and set aside.

Put the remaining butter in a skillet and melt over low heat. Meanwhile, peel and coarsely chop the pears, then add them to the skillet and cook, stirring gently, for 3 minutes. Stir in the toffee and continue to cook over low heat, stirring, for an additional 3 minutes.

Transfer the pear mixture to an ovenproof dish. Arrange the crumble evenly over the top, then sprinkle over the remaining sugar. Bake in the preheated oven for 25–30 minutes, or until the crumble is golden brown. Remove from the oven and serve with vanilla ice cream.

BAKED APPLES

Preheat the oven to 350°F/180°C. Using a sharp knife, chop the almonds very finely. Chop the apricots and preserved ginger very finely. Set aside.

Put the honey and ginger syrup in a pan and heat until the honey has melted. Stir in the oats and cook gently over low heat for 2 minutes. Remove the pan from the heat and stir in the almonds, apricots, and preserved ginger.

Core the apples, widen the tops slightly, and score around the circumference of each to prevent the skins from bursting during cooking. Place in an ovenproof dish and fill the cavities with the filling.

Pour just enough water into the dish to come about one third of the way up the apples. Bake in the preheated oven for 40 minutes, or until tender. Serve immediately.

Makes 4

1 tbsp blanched almonds

⅓ cup dried apricots

1 piece preserved ginger, drained, plus 1 tbsp syrup from the jar

1 tbsp honey

4 tbsp rolled oats

4 large baking apples

CREPES SUZETTE

Makes 8

Crepes

generous ¾ cup all-purpose flour

pinch of salt

2 tbsp superfine sugar

2 large eggs

1¼ cups milk

2 tbsp butter, melted and cooled

finely grated rind of 1 lemon

corn oil, for brushing

Orange sauce

¼ cup superfine sugar

1 tbsp water

finely grated rind of 1 large orange

½ cup orange juice

4 tbsp unsalted butter, diced

1 tbsp orange liqueur

2 tbsp cognac

To make the crepes, sift the flour, salt, and sugar into a large bowl and make a well in the center. Put the eggs and a little of the milk into the well and beat them together, gradually drawing in the flour. Stir in the butter, then slowly add the remaining milk until the batter has the consistency of light cream. Stir in the lemon rind. Cover and let stand for at least 30 minutes.

Heat an 8-inch/20-cm skillet over high heat, then lightly brush with oil. Reduce the heat to medium, add a ladleful of batter to the skillet, and swirl around so it covers the bottom thinly. Cook for 1 minute, or until the underside is cooked and golden. Use a spatula to flip over the crepe and cook on the other side. Transfer to a plate. Cook the remaining batter, stacking the crepes on the plate with parchment paper between each one.

To make the orange sauce, place the sugar in a wide sauté pan over medium heat and stir in the water. Continue stirring until the sugar dissolves, then increase the heat to high and let bubble for 1–2 minutes, or until it begins to turn golden brown. Stir in the orange rind and juice, then add the butter and stir until it melts. Add the liqueur.

Lay one of the crepes flat in the pan and spoon over the sauce. Fold the crepe into quarters and push to the side of the pan. Add the next crepe to the pan and repeat. Continue until all the crepes are coated with the sauce and folded. Remove the pan from the heat. Warm the cognac in a small pan, ignite, and pour over the crepes to flambé, shaking the pan. When the flames die down, serve the crepes with the sauce spooned over.

CRÈME BRÛLÉE

Prepare the berries, if necessary, and lightly rinse, then place in the bottoms of 4–6 x ⅔-cup ramekin dishes. Sprinkle the berries with the liqueur.

Cream the mascarpone cheese in a bowl until soft, then gradually beat in the sour cream.

Spoon the cheese mixture over the fruit, smoothing the surface and making sure that the tops are level. Chill in the refrigerator for at least 2 hours.

Sprinkle the tops with the sugar. Using a chef's blow torch, broil the tops for 2–3 minutes, or until caramelized. Alternatively, cook under a preheated broiler, turning the dishes, for 3–4 minutes, or until the tops are lightly caramelized all over.

Serve immediately or chill in the refrigerator for 15–20 minutes before serving.

Serves 4–6

8–10½ oz mixed mixed berries, such as blueberries and pitted fresh cherries

1½–2 tbsp orange liqueur or orange flower water

9 oz/250 g mascarpone cheese

1 cup sour cream

2–3 tbsp dark brown sugar

PAVLOVA

Serves 6

4 egg whites

1 cup superfine sugar

1 tsp cornstarch

1 tsp white wine vinegar

1 tsp vanilla extract

1¼ cups heavy cream

1 tbsp superfine sugar

2 tbsp framboise liqueur

1 cup fresh raspberries

2 oz/55 g semisweet chocolate shavings

Preheat the oven to 300°F/150°C.

In a large mixing bowl, using an electric mixer, beat the egg whites until stiff and gradually beat in a generous ½ cup of the sugar. In a separate bowl, mix the remaining sugar with the cornstarch, then beat it into the egg white mixture; it should be very shiny and firm. Quickly fold in the vinegar and vanilla extract.

Draw a 10-inch/25-cm circle on a sheet of parchment paper, turn the paper over, and place it on a cookie sheet. Pile the egg white mixture onto the baking paper and spread evenly to the edge of the circle; swirl it around on top to make an attractive shape. Bake in the center of the preheated oven for 1 hour.

Remove from the oven, let cool slightly, then peel off the parchment. Place the meringue on a large serving plate. It will shrink and crack, but do not worry about this.

Beat together the cream, sugar, and liqueur until thick and floppy. Pile on top of the meringue and decorate with raspberries and chocolate shavings. Chill in the refrigerator for 1 hour before serving.

LAYERED FRUIT DESSERT

To make the fruit layer, spread the ladyfingers with preserve, cut into bite-size pieces, and arrange in the bottoms of 4 individual serving dishes. Scatter over the fruit, pour over the sherry, and set aside.

To make the custard, put the cream and vanilla extract into a pan and bring almost to a boil over a low heat. Meanwhile, put the egg yolks and sugar into a bowl and beat together well. Remove the cream from the heat and gradually stir into the egg mixture. Return the mixture to the pan and warm over low heat, stirring, until thickened.

Remove the custard from the heat and let cool for 30 minutes, then pour it evenly over the fruit layer. Cover with plastic wrap and chill for 2½ hours.

Remove the dishes from the refrigerator. To make the topping, beat together the cream and sugar, then spread evenly over the custard layer. Cover with plastic wrap and chill for an additional 1½ hours. Sprinkle over the pistachios and decorate with strawberry halves just before serving.

Serves 4

Fruit layer

12 ladyfingers

2 tbsp strawberry preserve

6 large strawberries, hulled and sliced, plus extra strawberry halves to decorate

2 bananas, peeled and sliced

14 oz/400 g canned sliced peaches, drained

6 tbsp sherry

Custard layer

generous 1 cup heavy cream

1 tsp vanilla extract

3 egg yolks

4 tbsp superfine sugar

Topping

1¼ cups heavy cream

2 tbsp superfine sugar

chopped pistachios, to decorate

TIRAMISU

Serves 4

generous ¾ cup strong
black coffee, cooled to room
temperature

4 tbsp orange liqueur

3 tbsp orange juice

16 ladyfingers

9 oz/250 g mascarpone
cheese

1¼ cups heavy cream, lightly
whipped

3 tbsp confectioner's sugar

grated rind of 1 orange

2¼ oz/60 g chocolate, grated

chopped toasted almonds
and strips of lemon zest,
to decorate

Pour the cooled coffee into a pitcher and stir in the liqueur and orange juice. Put 2 of the ladyfingers in the bottom of each of 4 individual serving dishes, then pour over half of the coffee mixture.

Put the mascarpone in a separate bowl along with the cream, confectioner's sugar, and orange rind, and mix together well. Spread half of the mascarpone mixture over the coffee-soaked ladyfingers, then arrange the remaining ladyfingers on top. Pour over the remaining coffee mixture and then spread over the remaining mascarpone mixture.

Scatter over the grated chocolate and chill in the refrigerator for at least 2 hours. Serve decorated with chopped toasted almonds and strips of lemon zest.

BANANA & BROWN SUGAR RIPPLE DESSERTS

Preheat the oven to 375°F/190°C.

Toss the pecans in the superfine sugar, then scatter over a baking sheet and roast in the preheated oven for 4–5 minutes, or until golden. Remove from the oven and let cool, then coarsely chop.

Spoon the yogurt into a bowl and sprinkle the brown sugar evenly over the top. Let stand for 5 minutes, or until the sugar begins to melt, then fold it very lightly into the yogurt to create a rippled effect.

Peel and slice the bananas, then divide among 4 individual serving dishes. Carefully spoon over the yogurt, being careful to retain the rippled effect. Top with a scattering of the roasted pecans and serve immediately.

Serves 4

⅓ cup pecans

1 tsp superfine sugar

5 cups strained plain yogurt

3 tbsp dark brown sugar

3 ripe bananas

SYLLABUB

Serves 4–6

grated rind and juice of
1 lemon

½ cup sweet white wine

2 tbsp cognac

¼ cup superfine sugar

1 ¼ cups heavy cream

strips of lemon zest, to decorate

ladyfingers or ratafia cookies,
to serve

Place the lemon rind and juice in a bowl together with the wine and cognac. Cover and let steep for a few hours or overnight. Stir in the sugar until it has dissolved.

Beat the cream in a large bowl using an electric mixer. When it starts to thicken, carefully pour in the liquid, a little at a time, until it is all mixed in. The mixture should be very thick and soft; do not overbeat it. Spoon into small glasses and chill for a few hours. This can be made a day ahead.

Decorate with strips of lemon zest and serve with ladyfingers or ratafia cookies.

MANGO SHERBET

Using a sharp knife, thinly peel the mangoes, holding them over a bowl to catch the juices. Cut the flesh away from the central pit and put in a food processor or blender. Add the reserved mango juices, the lemon juice, and salt and process to form a smooth puree. Push the mango puree through a nylon strainer into the bowl.

Put the sugar and water in a heavy pan and heat gently, stirring, until the sugar has dissolved. Bring to a boil, without stirring, then remove from the heat and let cool slightly.

Pour the syrup into the mango puree and mix well. Let cool, then chill the mango syrup in the refrigerator for 2 hours, or until cold.

If using an ice-cream machine, churn the mixture in the machine following the manufacturer's instructions. Alternatively, freeze the mixture in a freezerproof container, uncovered, for 3–4 hours, or until mushy. Turn the mixture into a bowl and stir with a fork or beat in a food processor to break down the ice crystals. Return to the freezer and freeze for an additional 3–4 hours, or until firm. Cover the container with a lid for storing.

To serve, scoop into individual serving dishes and decorate with mango slices.

Serves 4–6

2 large ripe mangoes, plus extra slices to decorate

juice of 1 lemon

pinch of salt

generous ½ cup superfine sugar

3 tbsp water

AMARETTI TORTONI

Serves 6

4½ oz/125 g amaretti cookies

1¼ cups heavy cream

⅔ cup light cream

1 cup confectioners' sugar

4 tbsp Marsala

Line an 8 x 4 x 2-inch/20 x 10 x 5 cm loaf pan or 3½-cup oblong freezerproof plastic container with plastic wrap, allowing it to hang over the edges of the container so that the ice cream can be easily removed.

Put the cookies in a food processor and process to form fine crumbs. Alternatively, put the cookies in a strong plastic bag and crush with a rolling pin.

Pour the heavy cream and light cream into a large bowl and beat together until the mixture holds its shape. Sift the confectioners' sugar into the whipped cream, then fold in with the Marsala. Fold in the cookies, reserving one third.

Pour the mixture into the prepared pan or plastic container, smooth the surface, and freeze, uncovered, for 5 hours, or until firm. Cover the container with a lid for storing.

Take the ice cream out of the freezer about 30 minutes before you are ready to serve it. Uncover, turn out onto a serving dish, and remove the plastic wrap. Let stand at room temperature to soften slightly. Using a palette knife, press the reserved crushed cookies lightly onto the top and sides of the ice cream until it is evenly coated. Serve cut into thick slices.

HONEYCOMB ICE CREAM

Grease a baking sheet. To make the honeycomb, put the sugar and corn syrup in a heavy pan and heat gently until the sugar has dissolved, then boil for 1–2 minutes, or until beginning to caramelize, being careful not to let the mixture burn. Stir in the baking soda, then immediately pour the mixture onto the prepared baking sheet but do not spread. Let stand for about 10 minutes, until cold. When the honeycomb is cold, put it into a strong plastic bag and crush into small pieces using a rolling pin.

Beat the cream until it holds its shape, then stir in the condensed milk. If using an ice-cream machine, churn the mixture in the machine following the manufacturer's instructions. Just before the ice cream freezes, add the crushed honeycomb, reserving a little for decoration. Alternatively, freeze the mixture in a freezerproof container, uncovered, for 1–2 hours, or until it begins to set around the edges. Turn the mixture into a bowl and stir with a fork or beat in a food processor until smooth. Fold in the honeycomb pieces. Return to the freezer and freeze for an additional 2–3 hours, or until firm. Cover the container with a lid for storing.

To serve, scoop into individual serving dishes and decorate with the reserved crushed honeycomb.

Serves 6–8

butter, for greasing
scant ½ cup granulated sugar
2 tbsp dark corn syrup
1 tsp baking soda
1¾ cups heavy cream
1¾ cups canned sweetened condensed milk

Index